Tradition, Opinion, and Truth

Tradition, Opinion, and Truth

The Emerging Church of Christ

Fred Peatross

Writers Club Press

San Jose New York Lincoln Shanghai

Tradition, Opinion, and Truth
The Emerging Church of Christ

All Rights Reserved © 2000 by Fred Peatross

No part of this book may be reproduced or transmitted in any
form or by any means, graphic, electronic, or mechanical, including
photocopying, recording, taping, or by any information storage
retrieval system, without the permission in writing from the publisher.

Writers Club Press
an imprint of iUniverse.com, Inc.

For information address:
iUniverse.com, Inc.
620 North 48th Street, Suite 201
Lincoln, NE 68504-3467
www.iuniverse.com

ISBN: 0-595-13911-6

Printed in the United States of America

DEDICATION

It's with loving memories that I dedicate this book to my mother and my wife. I'm thankful that mom persevered and "stuck" with me during the years that I was difficult to love. Thank you Mom, for providing the direction I needed as a young man. In the summer of 1994, I immersed my mother into Christ. She left this earth to be with Jesus on December 31, 1994. I'm coming to see you!

And thank you to my wife who modeled Christ for me while I lived in the far land. It's because of her that my mother is home with God and I have a future in eternity with the two most influential people in my life. I love you both!

—Fred

EPIGRAPH

That with respect to the commands and ordinances of our Lord Jesus Christ, where the Scriptures are silent as to the express time or manner of performance, if any such there be, no human authority has power to interfere, in order to supply the supposed deficiency by making laws for the Church; nor can anything more be required of Christians in such cases, but only that they so observe these commands and ordinances as will evidently answer the declared and obvious end of their institution. Much less has any human authority power to impose new commands or ordinances upon the Church, which our Lord Jesus Christ has not enjoined. Nothing ought to be received into the faith or worship of the Church, or be made a term of communion among Christians, that is not as old as the New Testament.

That although inferences and deductions from Scripture premises, when fairly inferred, may be truly called the doctrine of God's holy word, yet are they not formally binding upon the consciences of Christians farther than they perceive the connection, and evidently see that they are so; for their faith must not stand in the wisdom of men, but in the power and veracity of God.

Therefore, no such deductions can be made terms of communion, but do properly belong to the after and progressive edification of the Church. Hence, it is evident that no such deductions or inferential truths ought to have any place in the Church's confession.

—Thomas Campbell

Declaration and Address published in 1809

CONTENTS

FOREWORD

From the very beginning, the church has had to face challenge after challenge. From Jerusalem, the message of Christ spread throughout every region of the world. There was no place it could not go. As the message spread across the cities, towns and regions, it caused a change in people that turned the world upside down.

As congregations of the Body of the Lord were born, they immediately began facing a multiplicity of trouble. There were those who denied that God really walked in the flesh. There were some who would not turn loose of the Law of Moses and follow the Christ of the New Covenant. There were false doctrines, real false doctrines, hidden in the hearts behind the faces of many who called themselves believers. The church faced mysticism, asceticism, Gnosticism and a host of other doctrines that threatened her heart. But, the most destructive and the most common problem was ritualism and traditionalism.

For many of the Jews, leaving the rituals and traditions of the elders was the unthinkable. Many of them wanted the "life" that Jesus promised, but could not commit to Him because of having to break with the rituals and traditions that had driven them for fifteen hundred years. They had become co-dependent on these values, to the point that many of them could no longer think for themselves. They were stuck...stuck between life and death...riches and poverty...religion and Christ, so that their hearts could not be moved to serve the Christ who died and was raised to give them life.

Today, the church is somewhat different. It is different in that it does not face the same kind of trouble our early brothers had. We skate past an issue here and there, but we do not face all of the false doctrines, grinding from day to day trying to make sense of God. But, the rituals and traditions have stayed around. We face them daily. And, like the Jews in the days of our early brothers, we too, have difficulty letting go of the past and pressing on to Christ.

Fred Peatross has challenged us with a book that should cause us to think about some things. Our traditions tell us to kill the "free thinker's" spirit...shut him down. Fred has moved from being co-dependent on rituals and traditions, and walked into the freedom of Jesus Christ.

We, too, can experience the freedom of Christ...but we must be willing to take a chance. We must be willing to challenge our faith, our teaching, and even our heritage. Fred has some thoughts that will help us help ourselves. Do not fear the challenge. If anything, we should fear the weakness of our faith. If it will not stand a challenge, perhaps it is centered in the wrong place instead of the right person, Jesus Christ.

Thank you Fred for sharing your thoughts and causing us to think.

Garry Knighton
Pulpit Minister
Church of Christ/ North
Shreveport, La.

PREFACE

To write concerning God's truth is a frightening proposition. Yet, that fear is multiplied when the Biblical ideas shared are different from the traditional views.

New expressions of truth that emphasize grace, and at the same time expose legalism, can play right into the hands of the brotherhood "watch-dogs." But that's the risk a truth-teller takes. It's at the very core of the grace-centered life. And it's worth all the potential harassment that can come from writing a book of this nature.

Too many believers are trapped in the "tradition box." It doesn't happen over night. It takes years and years of sitting in a pew and listening to the party's systematized theological statements. It's then that the teachings become so familiar that they seem as inspired as scripture itself. The Christian must be freed from the chains of party-ism.

This book is your compass. Read on!

-Fred Peatross

ACKNOWLEDGEMENTS

I acknowledge my debt to my Christian brother, but more importantly my friend, Chuck White for faithfully editing the manuscript.

A hearty thank you to all the subscribers to the "GraceAwakening"newletter who continue to remind me that what I am writing is touching them where they live.

LIST OF CONTRIBUTORS

A "heartfelt" thank you to Buff Scott, Jr. for allowing me to include a few of his thought-provoking articles. Buff, your thoughts have made this a better book.

INTRODUCTION

NO CHANGE WITHOUT PAIN

Buff Scott, Jr.

There's a secret to pushing someone's sore button. All you need do is rec-ommend change in his doctrinal position or theological stance. This seems to set off the alarm quicker than anything else. Rarely is there change without pain. For reasons of comfort, we prefer to remain where we are. This is called staying in our "comfort zone." Jesus the Messiah and John the Immerser fought for change. So did the old prophets before them. John's ministry of reformation got him beheaded. The same min-istry nailed Jesus to a Roman cross. The old reformers (prophets) were persecuted and many were put to death, and for no other reason than advocating change or reform.

Far be it from us to even think about placing our reformation min-istries on a par with Jesus, John, and the prophets of old. Our meager efforts don't even compare. But even with meager efforts, opposition lifts its ugly head. Most of the opposition comes from God's children of differ-ent persuasions. I mention this only to demonstrate the truth that we would rather "fight than switch." Change comes hard. It's never easy. The Jewish clergy in Jesus' day refused to reform. They had no intentions of abandoning their orthodox comfort zone.

And so it is with many religious leaders today. Times haven't changed all that much. They'll fight, resist, oppose, and obstruct before they'll change. Reformers don't let this discourage them. We believe that what we're doing is badly needed. Unless there's a general reformation of the entire religious establishment, we will in time "die on the vine." Death symptoms surround us. We've wandered, drifted, digressed, and become a stiff-necked people, very much like the Jews of old.

We harbor no hate in our hearts toward any of those who oppose our efforts. We love all of them. They are God's people and blood brothers and sisters of the Lamb. There's always the possibility our efforts at reformation are without heaven's blessings. In that case, we'll let our Lord and Savior determine our sincerity. But, whether our efforts receive God's blessing or not, there's one truth that all of us must in time accept. It is that if God doesn't raise up prophets (reformers) to bring His people back in line, we'll wind up on the back shelf of some ancient museum. I have confidence God will somehow correct the apostasy. We may have to be brought to our knees to see the problems at hand. So be it.

"Reform your ways and your actions…" (Jeremiah 7:3a).

Truth

NOT GOOD ENOUGH

In the early years of my Christian walk I was influenced and convinced that Christianity was a rule-bound spirituality that emphasized external conformity rather than an inner change of the heart. Keeping the party's elaborate system of rules was the evidence of my spirituality.

As I grew older in the faith I became aware of my desire to do more. I had been cleansed of my sins and saved by grace, but I still felt bad, as if I needed to do something more. I felt that no matter what I did or accomplished, it wasn't good enough. As I look back, I now realize that this was my first encounter with the inherited legalism of the church in which I grew up.

I continued to study the scriptures and as I did I began to see new truths. Many of my conclusions didn't parrot the traditional interpretations of the church of Christ. I soon realized that this legalistic Christian community I was converted in wasn't a safe place to share my doctrinal thoughts. It was obvious that if you shared your problems, difficulties, or dysfunction you faced the real possibility of judgment rather than love and support. Experience and observation taught me that the unwritten creed determined faithfulness and unfaithfulness, so I disciplined myself not to talk about the less-than-perfect things I did and the less-than-perfect things I thought. Shame-based, perfectionist theology forces you to "keep secrets" for fear of judgment. Conversations become limited to spiritualized small talk that reveals nothing about who you are or what you are going through. It majors in judgment and minors in grace. It puts the mask of religious perfection on your heart and enforces denial and causes the pain to go deeper only leading to dysfunctional families and churches.

You'll not find the church Jesus' died for in legalistic religion. You'll find it in a group of people called together by the vision of love found in Jesus. Sharing a common Father, born through a common new birth, held by a common Lord, they pursue a common course—the adventure of loving their neighbor as they love themselves.

As a sort of footnote, I would urge you, as did Jesus, to see through all the religious failure around you to the One who calls you out of that failure into a family of people who live by the standard of grace.

Remember, Jesus established the greatest adventure for persons the world has ever seen (a fact attested to by His enemies) and He did it in the midst of massive religious failure.

OWNING YOUR OWN INTERPRETATIONS

Let an independent thinker (one who owns his thoughts) challenge the accepted interpretation (party line) and the emotional rage is not unlike that which Jesus experienced when He challenged the religious establishment of His day.

Bertrand Russell said, "Every new idea starts out as blasphemy." New ideas will cause many to go to war to protect the system. There's no middle ground. You're either part of the system or your new ideas are a potential threat to that system.

When Jesus came proclaiming the Good News, He disturbed those who should have been looking for Him. Instead, they rejected Him and eventually murdered Him. For generations bold men, like Jesus, have altered the history of Christianity with their new ideas. Luther nailed his thesis to the door of the cathedral at Wittenberg. John Nelson Darby persistently taught in the face of a religious establishment that derided and condemned his teachings as the blather of an uneducated man. These men were pioneers not easily awed by the religious establishment. Moreover, they were men with whom today's religious establishment would feel very uncomfortable. New ideas start out as strange ideas. Few are willing to listen to an idea or concept that might require admitting wrong or a need to change.

An independent thinker knows that if his conclusions don't incorporate within the group's accepted interpretations, that he'll be considered a potential false teacher. It's a rare thing for an individual to own his own doctrinal beliefs. There have been some interesting studies done on groups of people who've taken on, or introjected an idea that doesn't belong to them. The more extreme will swallow the groups' teachings and will fight to the end to protect the system. When one listens from a programmed state it's not easy to recognize or accept new truth.

The religious establishment in Jesus' day had two concerns:

- Determining proper authority
- Applying the intent of Scripture to their lives

New Testament Christians have the same two concerns. Living in the midst of an ever-changing world, as the Pharisees did, we're forced to deal with contemporary religious problems that scripture doesn't specifically address. Both past and present concerns must be thought through, worked out, and harmonized using scriptural principles. These combined concerns and needs produced an authoritative oral law for the Pharisees. The same combined concerns and needs have produced an oral law for the churches of Christ. The Pharisee's oral law was "the tradition of the elders"; the oral law today is the "tradition of the preachers and teachers." The Pharisees, as well as we, have regarded faithfulness to their interpretations as equal with scripture. Considering that there are both good and bad interpretations makes this an impossible proposition for the independent thinker. Conjecture, uninformed opinion, informed opinion, educated opinion, convictions based on study, and convictions based upon research are all forms of interpretation. When we listen, over and over, to the same church of Christ interpretations, they become the establishment creed. Over time, these borrowed understandings (you don't own them, someone else taught them to you) become part of us. Thereafter, we listen to new ideas in a hypnotic state that's programmed to resist.

The churches of Christ need to allow free thinkers the freedom to think. Secondly, we need to develop a readiness to listen to the creative thinker without judging. The chances that the churches of Christ will move forward are in direct proportion to our willingness to listen to new interpretations of scripture without running away.

LIGHTING THE DARK TUNNEL OF LEGALISM

The critical issue in the churches of Christ isn't what we know about Jesus but that we know Him. Being religious without intimately knowing Jesus is like owning a Lexus without a motor. When anything but Jesus is made the issue, it tends to polarize rather than unify and Jesus' prayer in John 17 continues to go unanswered. Someone has said, "Whatever you make the issue, you make the idol."

It's an indisputable fact that Jesus is the critical issue. He made Himself the issue when He confronted Peter at Philippi with the fundamental question:

"Who do you say that I am?" Simon Peter answered, "You are the Christ, the Son of the living God." Jesus replied, "Blessed are you, Simon son of Jonah, for this was not revealed to you by man, but by my Father in heaven." (Matthew 16:15-17 NIV)

The apostle John, who wrote his first epistle to those "who believe on the name of the Son of God," was explicit as to the central issue when he defined the criterion:

"This is how you can know the Spirit of God: Every spirit that acknowledges that Jesus Christ came in the flesh is from God, but every spirit that does not acknowledge Jesus is not from God. (1 John 4:2-3 NIV)

It may surprise you to know that the first heresy in the church didn't deny the divinity of Jesus. Instead it denied Jesus' humanity and in doing so denied God's perfect model of humanness. This 1st-century issue dominated the church. The very essence of God's divine strategy was sacrificed to dogma. And with that a segment of God's people lost touch with the essential aspect of God identifying with mankind. Two thousand years later, dogma continues to be our primary approach to an unbelieving world. Instead of presenting the fascinating, irresistible Jesus, we present the rightness of our doctrine. And with pervasive skill we make another convert to religion. There are no tunnels darker than the tunnel of legalism. Its pitfalls are many and deep. The endless maze of channels is cluttered with the disoriented. Its paths are covered with split wineskins and spilled wine.

When those of new faith are taken into this tunnel, their questions quickly stale in the numbing darkness. Fresh insights are squelched in order to protect fragile traditions.

Christ had nothing but stinging words for those who live in the tunnels of legalism. "Hypocrites, white-washed tombs, snakes, vipers, blind guides." Jesus had little patience for those who made religion their idol.

Yet, have you noticed that just when the religious get too much religion God seems to find someone in the tunnel to light a candle? John Knox fanned the flame as a galley slave. Luther lit a candle at Wittenburg. And, today, the grace-centered churches are lighting the flame for those trapped in the tunnel.

It's not easy to light a candle in a dark tunnel. Yet, those whose lives have been illuminated with the Light of the Master know that a candle burns the brightest in the darkest of tunnels.

EVANGELISM IN AMERICAN CHURCHES OF CHRIST

Transition from the traditionalism of the 1960s, 1970s, and 1980s has produced and is still producing grace-oriented and Christ-centered churches of Christ. But transitions burn mega energy. The result is tired tree choppers and path clearers who have little energy left for further advancement of God's kingdom. We're poised and ready. But, what are we ready for?

- To continue telling the traditionalist to move on to the pews of "The One True Church" down the road?

- To continue practicing the unbiblical pastor system that should have went with the rest of the trash heap?

- To let the next generation take the reigns? Maybe soon, but what have we left them with?

The final chapter in our scroll should be the rekindling of the fires of evangelism. At one time we were the fastest growing church in America. Oh, I know we were converting people to something other than Jesus, but you have to admit that we, at the least, had an outward look.

I'm afraid that we are stuck in a transition that is essentially over for most of the churches of Christ. It's time to get our "getty-ups" moving! Souls are lost in the muck of a post-modern world and are looking for meaning and significance in all the wrong places. Have you noticed? Have you been listening? If you'll listen closely you'll hear a phrase that should cause those of us who know Christ to take notice.

"Right now I'm into..." The list is endless.

"Right now I'm into…" the stock market…exercising…Start listening and you'll be able to fill in the blank.

When it comes to evangelism, I'm convinced that we have some hurdles to jump in the grace-oriented churches of Christ. As Yogi Berra might say, "These are them."

- There are some who don't care about the lost and never will.

- There are those who care, but have never been taught how to win the lost.

- Realizing that God's kingdom may be broader than first believed, some are confused about who's saved and who's lost.

- There are those who know who needs the gospel, but they're not organized and there's no plan. They practice a voodoo evangelism. It's hit or miss. Mostly miss.

Churches today need to organize themselves around Jesus' Great Commission. Soul conscience leaders need to step forward and begin (even if it's a small start) training and organizing a group of men and women who care about the status of a person's relationship with the Master. Grace oriented, Christ-centered churches need leaders with a vision and a plan.

Unity in all of our diversity will be a reality when a body of believers starts converting souls on a weekly, daily basis. Then, and only then, will we be better equipped to see that all our issues are just that. They're issues. But, not until we start practicing and seeing the result of our commitment will we see and, then, understand what is important.

EVANGELISM AMONG THE GRACE-CENTERED: ITS CURRENT CRISIS

I don't care what they say; it's not like falling off a log. Leading a soul to Christ is time consuming and energy draining. If you're a task-centered person like me, dealing with people can be trying. I have told others that they could deliver two meals a day to my study and me and my three books and computer would do just fine. So, what am I saying? I'm admitting that I'm not the "evangelism type." But, even a guy like me, who's more at home with the second half of the Great Commission than the first half, has noticed the disappearance of evangelism from the grace-centered congregations.

I can remember a decade ago when evangelism flourished at the congregation where I attend. What I once thought was good, spiritual, and Christ-centered, I now realize was nothing more than a legalistic exercise of "t" crossing and "i" dotting. Then, I lived with a Bible in one hand and Ivan Stewart's four-part Bible study in the other. I convinced many gullible prospects that they had to climb the rungs of a works ladder to salvation. No longer do I use or even agree with Ivan Stewart's Open Bible Study (OBS). It's a tool of the patternist that emphasizes man's responsibility over what God has done through Jesus Christ. I'm glad the Lord has purged me of this type of personal evangelism. But, what has replaced it? What are we doing today a decade later, in the grace-centered churches of Christ? Are we seeking the lost or have we lost direction? Do we know who the lost are?

In the transitional period of the last decade, evangelism has crystallized into similar, but new forms. The "seeker movement" is but one example. We found that if we could survive all the complaining of the traditionalist, we could have an assembly that would attract the seeker by being

11

both culturally relevant and biblical. These efforts to attract and hold the seeker have caused us to move "personal evangelism" back to the platform for "attraction evangelism." Gradually, our emphasis has switched from winning souls to "growing churches." And most of the "growing" or "swelling" has been through crop rotation. Where bored boomers left their "less than relevant" churches for our more uplifting and motivating environments. Maybe we decided it was easier to get people to "come to church" than to get them saved?

Intriguing Evangelism

Through the years I have noticed that the best soul winners are those who have lived on both sides of the fence. It's not something I would recommend, but there's something to be said about what's developed in a person before his conversion to the Master. Maybe it's understanding and concern. Maybe it's the immediate reality of Jesus. I'm not sure what it is, but a new convert's obvious zeal keeps me fresh. I need these new Christians. They bring me back to center. They remind me that our calling transcends all our issues. Yet, watching these new disciples reminds me of a question I have for the Lord when I get to heaven. Why does He give us so much zeal when we're so young in the faith and so much wisdom years later after we've aged in the faith? Wouldn't it have been better to combine the two?

Today, somewhere in between "zeal without knowledge" and "wisdom without zeal," I've learned the value of stimulating the mind of my non-Christian friends. Could it be that developing curiosity is one of the most neglected aspects of evangelism today? In the past, I saturated people with the light before I ever had their attention. I find it interesting that Paul said Jesus called him to open the eyes of others before helping them turn from darkness to light (Acts 26:18). This is part of being a "fisher of men" rather than a "hunter of men." Maybe a brief look at Jesus and Paul's fishing techniques will help.

Jesus was often deliberately vague and intriguing with people at first, not giving the whole answer until He had their complete interest. He knew the Samaritan woman (John 4:7-42) wouldn't understand "living water" any more than Nicodemus would comprehend the term "born again" (John 3). Here deliberate obscurity was a stimulus of spiritual interest.

Paul aroused the curiosity of the Thessalonian Jews in the synagogue with his logic and rational arguments (Acts 17). In Athens, he captured the interest of the Greeks by citing their poets to affirm his points (Acts 17:28). He never aroused interest with a, "Gee, I dunno fellas, it's just this feeling in my heart."

We too need to develop an intriguing evangelism style that will pique the interest of our neighbors, coworkers, and friends.

BAPTISM AND ACTS 2:38

Acts 2:38, is a verse that's long been a favorite in the churches of Christ. I believe every word in that verse. At times our emphasis has caused the religious world to hear us preach a baptismal regeneration. Maybe if our emphasis had been on Jesus, the religious world would have listened to our exposition of Acts 2:38. After all, Jesus saves us. He's our salvation. Without Him baptism is no different than a summer dip in the river or a bath in a tub. Yet, I certainly want to be fair with the many in the churches of Christ who still think we need to pound others into baptism submission with Acts 2:38. As they say, "Been there, done that." As a new Christian I was usually the first one out the church building door with a Bible under my arm and "two axes and a 38" loaded for bear. My emphasis was doctrinal and my goal was to straighten others out. It didn't matter if you saw Jesus or came close to Him after ten minute with me.

Years later I still believe Acts 2:38. But, my emphasis has changed and there's been a recalibration of my hermeneutics. Jesus is now the center.

On the day of Pentecost, Peter told those in the crowd that gathered to, "Repent and be baptized, every one of you in the name of Jesus Christ for the forgiveness of your sins. And you will receive the gift of the Holy Spirit." (Acts 2:38)

There was a time when I taught that a person had to understand that their baptism was for "the forgiveness (remission) of sin" or their baptism was invalid. But, recalibration has caused me to ask a couple of questions? What is the command in Acts 2:38? The command is "be baptized." What is the promise? The promise is you will receive "forgiveness (remission) of sins."

Think with me for just a minute. Would you agree that we obey commands? Of course we do. Do we obey promises? You know as well as I do that that's not even possible. The promise is the result of obeying the command. The logical conclusion is that anyone who obeys the command to "be baptized" will receive what God has promised whether he is cognizant of it or ignorant of it.

Emphasis makes all the difference.

CHRISTIANITY'S GREATEST CHALLENGE- POSTMODERN DIVERSITY

The five hundred year period of history that Martin Luther started, the era we know as the modern era, the era of Enlightenment, has come to an end. Today we live in a post-modern culture.

The modern world embraced science and was characterized by trust in reason: which made doubt the basic spiritual problem. The post-modern world, unlike the modern world, embraces astrology, the New Age, gurus, miracles, and angels. No longer is it necessary to argue the case for spiritual realities. Doubt is no longer our spiritual problem. Today we need to help people believe the right thing.

Our challenge is to claim this moment for Christ. It's a unique moment that calls for unique strategies, skills, and sensibilities.

The Amish decided not to live their moment in history. They aren't taking any cues from the current culture. Their culture is frozen in the 1830s. They talk like it and dress like it.

God has chosen us to live in this place and time and He wants us to plant our feet in this moment of history and claim it for Christ. The question yet to be answered is what moment in history will the churches of Christ choose to live in?

When Jesus prayed in John 17, He prayed that the Father would keep His disciples in the world, but that they would not become of the world. So we are to be "in," not "of," and "not out of," the world. The church today needs to be in touch but not in tune with our culture.

Our time in history, in some ways, is facing as radical an upheaval as it did 150 years ago when Charles Darwin released his "Origin of the Species" and altered the thinking of the scientific world. At the time

Christians had no idea what was happening. But today everyone understands the far-reaching results of that revolution. Now, western culture embraces Darwin's theory of naturalistic evolution as if it was fact. The Christian church wasn't ready for Darwin.

Today we are caught up in another revolution that will likely dwarf Darwinism in its impact on culture and thought. Postmodernism is confusing, just as Darwin's evolving ideas were. It's presently causing a culture metamorphosis-transforming every area of life as it spreads through education and media. The Christian church is ill prepared for the challenges of postmodernism.

The following is a simplistic defining of the contrasting characteristics of the worldviews of Christianity, modernism, and postmodernism.

Modernism said-Stand up for what is right.

Postmodernism says-Allow tolerance (The Postmodern password is—"whatever").

Modernism said-To value order and structure.

Postmodernism says- Accept chaos and anarchy. Break down hierarchy.

Modernism said-Emphasize truth.

Postmodernism says-Emphasize impression, charisma and style (especially fashion).

Modernism said-Practice systematic thinking.

Postmodernism says-Believe what you like.

Both worldviews reject Jesus Christ. Compare the Christian worldview with modern and postmodern worldviews.

Christian-There is an Author.

Modern-There is no author, but there are ideals.

Postmodern-There is no author and no ideals.

Christian-We live in a grand story, the triumph of God's plan.

Modern-We live in a grand story, the triumph of reason, evolution, and the progress of the human spirit.

Postmodern-There is no grand story.

Christian-We have hope.

Modern-We are making progress (false hope).

Postmodern-We have no hope.

Like it or not, we have to take cultural trends seriously. This is the world that Christ died for, and this is the world He calls us to claim.

IDENTIFIABLE DISTINGUISHABLE MARKS

"...for I bear on my body the scars that show I belong to Jesus"
(Galatians 6:17)

I don't believe Jesus burned wounds into Paul's hands or feet. Yet, Paul had plenty of scars that attested to his faithfulness. Stuff happens when you follow Jesus. Sometimes that "stuff" can be the branding of the identifiable distinguishable marks of a servant of the Lord.

But I wonder, "How about you and me?" Do we bear the scars of Jesus? If not, have I really identified with the Savior?

When church leaders decided that they could promote (via corporate America's idea of public relations) the cross of Christ to the world they allowed humanism to enter their thinking. The cross is a negative bloody sacrifice. It's not possible for the church to promote the paradox of a cross to a world lost in their misunderstanding. The world despises the realities of Jesus. They would rather talk about "baby Jesus" at Christmas than discuss Jesus' supreme moment. They would rather talk about his nonviolent stance and the miracles He performed, but not the demands that a cross makes on each of us.

A Christian's spiritual enlightenment allows him to understand the nails in the hands and feet. It was that historical moment when man killed God. Two thousand years later, I still feel the nails, not in a physical sense, but in a deeply spiritual way.

It's not easy for the ones who love Jesus to try and feel the pain He must have felt when those of our race murdered Him. Like you, I cringe and want to look away. It hurts to look at His pain. But maybe it's supposed to hurt. Maybe I need to hurt more often...in order to be changed, transformed into His image.

LEADERSHIP STYLE

When Moses was leading Israel through the wilderness, he had to move at the speed of the slowest sheep. With slow lambs you have three choices: (1) abandon them, (2) pick them up and carry them, or (3) move at their speed.

Some churches choose not to lose any sheep and, therefore, allow the hurting lambs to determine the pace and sometimes the direction of the whole flock. Other churches feel that the direction and destination of the flock is a higher priority than the needs of every individual, so they carry those they can and admit they can't meet the needs of others.

Spiritual leaders are confronted regularly with such issues as serious health problems, disintegration of marriages, unemployment, suicides, sexual abuse, chemical dependence, or business failure. The list is endless.

Sensitive spiritual leaders attempt to enfold a person with attention until the problem is solved. After all, we're family! But, when the week is over, and we take inventory, we find that two or three individuals consumed all our time. Should leadership focus on the needs of a few or the needs of the body as a whole?

Someone has said that a person is adequately cared for when he or she perceives that (1) "Someone in church leadership loves me," and (2) "If I need attention, I can get it without feeling guilty." These two conditions seem like reasonable and reachable goals considering the overwhelming individual needs in a congregation.

The paradox is that churches lead by ministers who are "pastoral types" generally don't grow, and you can't grow unless you care for people. If a church becomes a spiritual hospital, focused primarily on bandaging wounds, then it tends not to develop the muscular faith necessary to engage our postmodern world with the gospel. Sometimes it seems as if pastoral care and visionary leadership are incompatible.

ELDERS, THEIR FAMILIES AND A THEOLOGICAL FINE TUNING

The families of preachers, elders, and deacons are expected to be role models. But, what are leaders and their families to model? For far too long we've measured effectiveness and competency by a *perfectionist* model when, in reality, the measuring of leadership should be based on a *confessional* model. Jesus gives us a picture of the confessional model in Luke 18. In this parable the publican admits his needs and faults rather than hiding them. The Pharisee does just the opposite and denies his faults. This parable ought to give leaders, preachers, elders, and every family the right and freedom to say, "We have struggles, fights, losses, and unanswered questions. We don't love each other all the time like we should, but we survive because we admit (confess) this and pray for each other."

Yes, leaders are to be "role models" but we can't pretend to be Jesus incarnate. If we do, we're as guilty as the Pharisee who prayed as if he had no problems. We are only frail representatives of Christ.

One of our "role model" passages that needs some theological fine-tuning is 1 Timothy 3:4-5.

"...He must manage his own family well and see that his children obey him with proper respect. If anyone does not know how to manage his own family, how can he take care of God's church?"

I want to key in on this phrase "must manage his own family well" (NIV) "manages his own household well" (NAS). What does "well managed" mean? Do we interpret this to mean immaculate and eliminate every man from shepherding God's people? This is not what Paul was trying to convey. "Well managed," doesn't mean "well-behaved" or even that a prospective elder's children must be visibly involved in the church. In this passage Paul deals with basic character traits, not the way every episode of life "has" to turn out. "Well managed" refers not so much to a result as it does to the importance of entering into the parental process and shouldering the responsibilities of the job.

Both Eli and Samuel had disappointing results with their children. Yet, Jehovah punished Eli for his ineffective parenting and blessed Samuel, who shouldered his responsibility, even though he had an unfortunate result. If a prospective leader is trying to be a "good father" and hasn't shirked his God-given responsibility, yet his children don't "turn out", is he a Samuel? On the other hand, if the father irresponsibly ignores his parental duties, with a predictable result, is he an Eli?

"Well managed" is the faithful process of parenting, not the end result. It's time we begin distinguishing between the self-destructive behavior brought on by poor parenting and the developmental crisis that teenagers predictably pass through. For too many years we've eliminated good, godly men who've desired to lead Gods people!

WOULD YOU FELLOWSHIP THE FOLLOWING MEN?

The dynamics of our faith should lead us to a more increasingly balanced doctrinal stance on the issues within the heritage known as the churches of Christ. There are some quotes on this page you may not endorse. Yet, the question is not, "do we agree with them," but would we allow these pioneers of the past to stand in our pulpits today?

- **Barton Stone**

  "I see no authority in the Scriptures as to why we should draw the conclusion, that the miraculous gift of the Holy Spirit, is withdrawn from the church."

- **Alexander Campbell**

  "We, as a denomination are as desirous as ever to unite and cooperate with all Christians on the broad and vital principles of the New and everlasting Covenant."

  "It is the image of Christ the Christian looks and loves; and this does not consist in being exact in a few items, but in general devotion to the whole truth as far as known."

  "But who is a Christian? Everyone that believes in his heart that Jesus of Nazareth is the Messiah, the Son of God; repents of his sin, and obeys him in all things according to his measure of knowledge of his will."

  "I cannot make any one duty the standard of Christian state or character, not even immersion."

"In our furious zeal for orthodoxy, we have made baptism a savior, or a passport to heaven, disparaging all private and social virtues of the professing public."

"We do not suppose all unimmersed persons to be absolute aliens from the family of God-nor are they absolutely excluded from any participation with us in prayer or in the Lord's Supper."

"All the good and virtuous in all sects belong to Jesus Christ; and if I belong to him, they are my brethren."

- **Thomas Campbell**

"You may possibly infer from these remarks that I make immersion essential to salvation. By no means: for mistakes in such cases are pardonable. God judges people on the basis of the available light they possess."

"That although inferences and deductions from Scripture premises, when fairly inferred, may be truly called the doctrine of God's holy word, yet they are not formally binding upon the consciences of Christians farther than they perceive the connection, and evidently see that they are so; for their faith must not stand in the wisdom of men but in the power of God."

- **Robert Richardson**

"Let the Bible be our spiritual library; but let the gospel be our standard of orthodoxy."

"Christ is not a doctrine but a person."

"People may possess the same faith, while they differ greatly in the amount and accuracy of their religious knowledge."

- **David Lipscomb**

"When I hear of a church setting out to build a fine building, I give that church up. It's usefulness as a church of Christ is at an end."

Concerning preacher salaries: "The preacher will cater to his supporters."

- **Moses E. Lard**

  "Phoebe was a deaconess in the official sense of that word...whenever the necessities of the churches are such as to demand it, the order of the deaconess should be reestablished."

- W.K. Pendelton

  "It is generally regarded among our brethren, as an essential element in the restoration of the primitive order, to ordain, in every church, both deacons and deaconesses."

- T.B. Larimore

  "I propose never to stand identified with one special wing, branch, or party of the church. My aim is to preach the gospel, do the work of an evangelist, and teach God's children how to live."

- G.C. Brewer

  "Christians have made the gospel a system of divine laws for human beings to obey and thus save themselves sans grace, sans mercy, sans everything spiritual and divine-except the plan was in mercy given."

  "To trust a plan is to expect to save yourself by your own good works. It is to build according to a blueprint; and if you meet the specifications the great Inspector will approve your building. Otherwise you fail to measure up and you are lost. That is wrong, brethren! We have a Savior who saves us. We throw ourselves upon his mercy, put our case in his hands, and submit gladly and humbly to his will. That is our hope and our only hope"

- **K.C. Moser**

  "If we are saved by a plan, does this make the plan our savior? Is there life in a plan? Is a plan redemptive? Jesus thought that he died to save sinners. If he died to give us a plan by which to be saved, then it is not his death by which we are saved, but the plan given by reason of his death."

"What this sinful world needs is not plans and schemes but Christ. When Christ crucified is not preached one should not preach at all."

- **Charles Loos** (A Restoration forefather and teacher at Bethany College)

"Doctrines do not save us; we are saved by Christ. Doctrines do not cleanse us from our sins; it is the efficacious blood of Christ. We are not converted to doctrines, but to God…We are not baptized into doctrines, but into Christ. We do not hope in them, trust in them, glory in them, but in Jesus Christ our Lord."

- **John T. Johnson** (*In a letter to Alexander Campbell, 1849*)

"Were it not for the preachers, Christians would unite upon the Bible alone in less than one year, in my judgment."

CONFORMITY AND ITS DEMANDS VS.
THE FREEDOM OF DIVINE UNITY?

When an individual does what the Bible says to do to become a Christian he is a Christian. He doesn't need to know me, or my group and he doesn't need to know you and your group. He just needs to know Jesus.

When one considers all those right-brain (emotionally guided) and left-brain (logically guided) folks in our brotherhood and then you mix them with the type A personality (here come da judge) and the type B personality (let it slide Clyde), we have to give God all the credit for keeping things together the way he has. Mix in a thousand years of culture blending, wars, ignorance, learning, fear, hope, weak, and charismatic personalities and it really is remarkable that we're as close in our thinking and practice as we are. A small segment of believers have had to study hard to divide the masses as effectively as they have been divided! We all understand the problem division can cause in the body of Christ, but few understand the divine unity and oneness taught in the New Testament. There are those who've equated unity with conformity. Yet conformity is not divine unity. At it's worst it's religious anarchy!

Unity in diversity is the only kind of unity possible. We have moved so far from the original restoration plea that most of our pioneer preachers would not be allowed in our pulpits today. The millennial views that Alexander Campbell and David Lipscomb embraced in the early 1800s are certainly not mainstream views today within the churches of Christ. Yet, diversity allowed Campbell and Lipscomb to hold those views without the fear of being disfellowshipped.

The Bible doesn't give us blueprints or specific instructions as to how to seek unity. Neither did the apostle Paul give us a how to manual. Thinking is required. So use your imagination and be creative! I have decided that common sense would at least tell us that goodwill, motivated by the love of Jesus and the hope of the empty tomb would be enough instruction. Today would not be too soon for us to realize that the Spirit creates unity. We maintain it, recognize it, and appreciate it. The concept I find in the New Testament for unity revolves around the attitude of humility. Being willing to adjust to differences with others through the actions of meekness and patience. These active qualities will not fit well in a heart filled with pride. And they interface even worse if we believe that conformity equals unity.

When we become serious about our splintered movement we will discard the eternal judgments we are guilty of attaching to our statements of conviction on non-salvation issues. Grace covers all my sin and all my misunderstandings. It covers much more than we've been willing to admit, both in our own lives and the lives of those we think are wrong. Besides, we're all wrong teachers.

As fellow-believers the Holy Spirit encourages us to make every effort to preserve the oneness He creates. In a word, you're Holy Spirit bound to your brother and sisters. It makes no difference if your group is instrumental, non-instrumental, premillennial, or non-institutional. For everyone who has named the name of Jesus is my brother.

LOGIC CHOPPERS

Years ago I made an attempt to become a self-taught garage mechanic. It only took a tune-up and a couple of oil changes for me to understand how essential it is to have the proper tools. I remember the time I accidentally got a metric nut jammed into a half-inch SAE socket wrench and was never able to punch it out and use that tool again.

Humanly speaking, we may have a preference for the kind of tools we employ when we approach scripture. If however, we utilize the wrong tools, frustration and ineffectiveness may be the result. Like when I jammed that metric nut into my SAE socket. Far more serious is the use of a tool of interpretation of scripture that isn't clearly scriptural. This faulty tool will take you beyond the limitations of ineffectiveness and frustration. My vehicle eventually returned to the road. But, in the church, we're not nearly as concerned about the right tools as is a garage mechanic. We need to use God's tools in examining His Word, not because we'll avoid delays and frustrations, but because this is the way to handle His Word correctly. When problems due to using a human tool of interpretation result in division, which God's Word clearly and categorically condemns, we need to take a hard look at our rules of interpretation.

There's nothing wrong with reason and logic, when the procedures are correct and they're kept outside the "doctrines and commandments of men." Our Lord Himself gave, on occasions, beautiful formal syllogisms when dealing with the scribes and Pharisees. These were people who loved to chop logic and it was highly appropriate for Jesus to beat them at their own game. Today, those who resort to this procedure aren't disposed to honoring the reasoning of others, or to accept the inevitable conclusion of the opposition's syllogisms. Often arguments that may seem crystal clear to us, so evident that one couldn't imagine another taking exception, are rejected by those who are challenged.

The blind man of John 9, when offered an argument against Jesus, gave us that magnificent statement, "Once I was blind, but now I see." But, Jesus' enemies wouldn't let it go at that. So, the blind man took on the logic choppers and fed them right through their own grinder. What did they do? They did what they had threatened to do with the blind man's parents. They kicked him out of the synagogue. This example, combined with what the logic choppers did to Jesus, shows how human reasoning, when challenged, tested, and rejected, can become very unreasonable.

Those who appeal to logic, as with those who resort to the sword, take the chance of being destroyed by logic.

Unity versus the Party Spirit

By: Buff Scott, Jr.

A fellow traveler who is party to one of our many factions said, "Anyone who teaches other than that which is clearly revealed in the Scriptures is a false teacher." He added, "If he does not surrender his false teachings, he is a heretic and should be treated as one."

It's safe to say that as long as this good brother demonstrates this kind of unyielding attitude, he will remain separated from God's other children. He categorizes as heretical anyone whose views run counter to his party's doctrinal platform. He is a good man, a supportive husband, and a loving father. He is a graduate of one of "our" colleges and has served in the capacity of pulpit minister and elder for many years. And, his sincerity has never been in doubt. But, his idea of oneness hinges on absolute conformity to his party's understanding of biblical doctrine. He is convinced that his church is the one ushered in by Jesus Christ and that anyone who resists his view of what Jesus set in motion is in danger of being lost. According to his conception of Jesus' plan, there can be no unity until all others give up what they have and join him and his bunch.

In spite of all this, I still consider this man a beloved brother in Jesus Christ. He is a beloved brother because he and I have the same Father, and he truly feels his concepts are in harmony with the divine testimony. He doesn't fit the biblical definition of a "false teacher," for he is not teaching false doctrine knowingly and deliberately.

But again, I esteem him as a beloved brother because at one time I was as he-sincere and zealous, but sincerely and zealously wrong. I was like Alexander Campbell described himself in his partisan days. He remarked that he was once so strong a separatist that he would neither pray nor sing with another unless they were as perfect as he knew himself to be. He persisted in this most unpopular course, he said, until he realized that if his position were sound, there could never be a congregation of saints on earth.

Sooner or later we all most come face-to-face with Campbell's conclusion. For if everyone else must arrive at our level of intelligence and attain our degree of biblical knowledge before unity can be realized, the one body of believers will always be divided.

My hunch is that at one time all of us were like Campbell in that we were spiritual adolescents—growing, maturing, reaching out, prodding, grasping, and learning. Some of us found greener pastures and higher plains while others fought growth and remained adolescents and slaves to the status quo. If those of us who no longer succumb to partisan shackles had resisted growth and change, we too would be parroting the party line.

But, free or enslaved, we have the same Father and that is all the more reason why we should lay aside our pride and reach out and grasp the hand of our brother as a gesture of comradeship and mutual concern. We of the Restoration heritage have so many majestic things in common that it's a shame and disgrace to remain divided over such trivial matters as musical forms, missionary societies, the millennium, and a host of other "adolescent issues."

So, what causes the divisive spirit among us? Is it not a matter of allegiance? For if our allegiance is placed in some party, or in some journal, or in some church, or in some city, or in some headquarters, we will never unite. We will simply continue our efforts to hoist our factional flags and solicit prestige for our competing splinters. The Corinthian believers were faced with the same problem. The allegiance of some was placed in Paul, others were devoted to Peter, and still others had given themselves to Apollos. Although not physically separated, they were nonetheless intellectually divided, insofar as allegiance was concerned. The Restoration brotherhood is not only divided in the matter of allegiance, but it is physically separated as well. And in that vein our plight is even worse than the plight of the Corinthians. We have anchored our allegiance in the wrong persons, in the wrong parties, pitched our tents in the wrong direction, and set our affections on the wrong journals. And all the while our heartstrings should have been attached to things above.

I like the way the apostle Paul expresses it: "Set your affections on things above, not on things below" (Colossians 3:2). To "set our affections" is to place our allegiance, our mind, and our thoughts on things above. The Living Bible hits home by saying that heaven should fill our thoughts. But how can this be when our time, our efforts, and our ventures are spent on increasing the size and reputation of the party? Let it forever be said that our parties will never achieve unity. They will, as they always have, only create more and more division. Where the party spirit makes its abode there is always schism. But, where the Holy Spirit is permitted to take the lead, there is tranquility—even in the face of persecution.

I'd like to remind my fellow heirs that the former Restoration Movement, begun by the Campbells, the Stones, the Smiths, and the Scotts, was non-sectarian initially. However, in time it became partisan and divided. At the outset, it cut across sectarian lines. Unity was on the upswing and thousands were being drawn toward the cross and away from partisan entanglements. It was a glorious genesis, and remained so until its adherents commenced placing allegiance in parties, projects, and organizations. The result has been about two-dozen splintered groups with each laying claim to heaven's blessings to the exclusion of all rival groups.

So we're back where the Campbells began. There are no more inroads into sectarian encampments. And that's because we've become as sectarian as those we hope to deliver from sectarianism! The solution, as I see it, is to cast aside every partisan shackle and reset our allegiance on things above. We either allow our allegiance to Jesus and to the divine testimony to supplant our divisions or we go on dividing until we become extinct. A divided front cannot overcome our archenemy, Satan. But a united front, with Jesus as Captain and the Holy Spirit as Counselor, can surge on to beat down all barriers and defeat all obstacles. If some prefer to be left behind to wallow in the ashes of Phariseeism, that is their choice. As for me and my house, we will press forward—so help us God.

BRANDING OUR BROTHERS

BY: BUFF SCOTT, JR.

Of all the passages of Scripture used by the disciples of the Restoration Movement to disown and divide God's sheep, this one is among the most widely engaged. The KJV says to "mark" and avoid them.

Paul's injunction has been employed as a "sword of the Spirit" to rip apart honest saints who entertain "wrong views" on instrumental music in the corporate assembly, Bible classes, communion cups, premillennialism, cooperative endeavors such as missionary and benevolent societies, the Herald of Truth radio and TV program, hats, and long hair. Irrational interpretations have been formulated and hierarchical action taken against good and contrite believers by those who have understood Paul's admonition to mean that unity can be attained only by dividing.

No religious party can exit for long without rigid standards. And those standards can't be enforced upon others or used as divisive weapons unless some Scripture is made to teach that division is the answer to our already divided movement. Thus conquering the human spirit, which dares to differ, is the only way to maintain the system.

Rank division occurred when we demonstrated to the world that we would rather build walls than bridges. The end result is that we have twenty or more partisan cliques within the "brotherhood" with each claiming to have a monopoly on truth and heaven hereafter. Most of these groups feel they've encompassed the whole body of truth and that others are depraved, divisive, and teachers of falsehood because they "do not bring this doctrine" (2 John 9-10). These factions contend that unity can only be achieved by joining them. And each group designates their party "the church of our Lord!" Surely an injustice is committed against Ephesians 4:4, where Paul makes it clear that there is one body of believers—one whole body, not split, severed, or separated.

There are valid reasons to believe that the "doctrine" Paul referred to is altogether alien to our contemporary issues, and contains no principle to deal with them. Even assuming that his "doctrine" provides a blueprint for our brotherhood problems, we would be compelled to brand or "mark" every brother and sister who disagrees with us on any and all subjects, since each of us considers our views major and important.

When Paul was faced with the wretched doctrinal condition of the Christian community at Corinth, he neither "marked" nor excommunicated them. Rather, he called them brethren and saints, and even addressed his epistle to the "congregations of God."

Was he concerned? Yes. Did he take corrective action? Indeed. But not in the form of excommunicative edicts, except in the case of the incestuous brother. Nor did he call upon other congregations to "mark" and avoid them. In fact, he did just the opposite. He told them that the congregations in the province of Asia send their greetings (1 Corinthians 16:9). He didn't direct the "faithful "saints to pull out and go to the other side of town and start a "sound church!" Instead, he initiated a program of love and concern. Positively stated, their problems were solved by their remaining and working together and loving one another.

Why didn't Paul use the principle most factions claim is found in Romans 16:17 and "mark" and "avoid" the Corinthian believers? If he could tell others to use it, why not be consistent and use it himself? I suggest that if "doctrine" in the passage under study alludes to anything not specifically mentioned in scripture, thus enveloping all of our theological hang-ups, there is no hope for unity among believers. Thus Jesus prayed a useless and meaningless prayer in John 17. Of course I'm not ready to accept this conclusion. I don't believe our Lord prayed for an impossible goal.

What did Paul mean in Romans 16:17? Let me paraphrase his statement.

"I beg you, my brothers, watch out for those who take pleasure in dividing God's children, for all of you have been taught that division is contrary to the doctrine which condemns it."

Notice that individual action, as opposed to congregational action, is stressed. The dividers were to be shunned, avoided, observed, and ignored "for such people are not serving our Lord Jesus Christ, but their own appetites. By smooth talk and flattery they deceive the minds of naïve people." (verse 18) These people were controlled by the part spirit of Galatians 5:20, and knowingly and deliberately attempted to separate God's sheep from the corporate fold and start a party or faction of their own making.

It's difficult for me to accept the notion that those brothers who believe it's admissible to play instruments of music in group worship are trying to deceive the minds of innocent people or serving their own partisan appetites, even though I personally prefer vocal music only in the assembly of the saints. Nor do I believe our "premillennial brethren" are heretics and striving to divide the family of God. Simply put, the doctrine I've learned is that God's people are not to be divided. This seems to be the central truth of the passage. Thus, those who are always accusing other brethren of "going beyond the doctrine of Christ," and who avoid and "mark" those who disagree with them, are the actual dividers, regardless of their sincerity. The "markers" are those who need to be "marked." Watch out for them, avoid them, and shun them, for their partisan nature demands division.

Love and tolerance will reunite God's children. The partisan spirit that marks all who differ will drive us further apart.

EVIDENCES

A skeptic once said, "Believers are offended when asked why they believe in Christianity because the awkward truth is that they have no reason, they just have a feeling." But there is ample evidence for believing Christianity to be true. Just listen and look at the evidence through the years.

Foreknowledge of Medical Science in the Bible

If you lived in Europe during the Middle Ages, you would have been at risk of contacting cholera, typhoid, leprosy, or the bubonic plague. These diseases were prevalent because garbage and sewage were allowed to lie in the streets and became the breeding grounds for rats and flies, which were the carriers that killed millions. Strange thing, the Jews rarely contacted these killer diseases. Why? Because they practiced the laws of sanitation found in the Bible. It wasn't until the church introduced the practice of quarantine (as taught in the Bible) and the cities turned to sewage disposal (as taught in the Bible) that these diseases were brought under control.

DESIGN

The thinking nonbeliever holds the view that life originated by chance. Chance is the enemy of design. Everyone understands that it takes intelligence, knowledge, and work to design a bridge or building. Structures and mechanisms don't just happen by chance. There's a fabulously complex structure and mechanism within the human body. The DNA molecules in your cells contain the necessary information for both growth and function within the human body. These instructions would fill several sets of the Encyclopedia Britannica. It would be more logical to believe that a set of encyclopedias was the result of an explosion in a print shop than to believe that the DNA system came about by mere chance. There is a great Biochemist!

RADAR AND SONAR

Men invented radar in the 1930s. This was an important invention and aided the defensive systems of the Allied forces during World War II. Bats, however, were equipped with radar long before man built the first system. Wouldn't it be illogical to believe that the bat's "natural" radar system is the result of chance and time, while knowing that electronic radar was the end result of intelligent and planning?

UNLEARNED KNOWLEDGE AND ABILITIES

Consider the unlearned abilities of birds. The meadowlark and starlings navigate by the sun. Geese and European warblers use the stars. Either system requires an inborn clock that has the ability to keep track of time. In order for man to travel, he must rely on finely tuned instruments. The bird, by design, has this ability. Isn't it more logical to believe that a compass or a clock could come into existence by accident than to believe that the navigational system in birds came about purely by chance? Maybe the truth is that when the evidence is weighed, it's more reasonable to believe in creation.

WHERE DID EVERYTHING COME FROM?

BUFF SCOTT, JR.

One morning as I was out walking I took a shortcut through a junkyard. About halfway through, I heard a big bang. Thousands of pieces of junk, small and large, began flying about me in a disorderly fashion. There was utter confusion. When order finally arrived, I looked down and there at my feet lay a shiny new wristwatch-band and all. During the commotion, numerous pieces of metal merged and formed what I now wear on my left wrist. Other pieces of metal fashioned additional items, all exquisite and perfectly shaped. And all of this was a result of the big bang.

You probably doubt my story, don't you? You'll likely reply, "There's no design without a designer, no product without a manufacturer, no drawing without an artist, no painting without a painter, no invention without an inventor. Therefore, your "big bang" didn't happen." I agree. It's the same principle with the universe and everything in it-including we humans.

The universe is a vast array of heavenly bodies, each functioning in its own orderly fashion. Truly, then, the universe is a design, a plan, and a creation. But, since there can be no design without a designer, no plan without a planner, or no creation without a creator, we're forced to conclude that the universe is the product of a supernatural Designer-God. As the opening line of the Bible announces: "In the beginning (of time) God created the heavens (universe) and earth" (Genesis 1:1).

ASCRIBE ALL WONDERS TO DEITY

These ancient affirmations say nothing about a "Big Bang" creation. There's nothing wrong with believing the "Big Bang" theory (and it's only a theory) as long as we ascribe it to Deity. We don't know the precise mechanics of our universe and its creation. We only know that Deity is the author.

What about all of the so-called scientific "evidence" that points to a "Big Bang?" Scientific "findings" must coincide with Deity's testimony, not the reverse. When we try to force Deity's testimony to harmonize with our scientific views and theories, we place ourselves on a level above the Creator. Heaven's declarations make no reference to a "Big Bang," directly or indirectly. So, it must remain a theory until scientists are able to prove without a doubt that the universe is the result of a "Big Bang." We would then be compelled to ascribe the phenomenon to Deity-not to chance, not to a haphazard occurrence, and not to godless evolution. For those whose "scientific knowledge" attributes nothing to Deity in the forming of our universe, think about this: Why did the "Big Bang" fashion only round planets. Why not a few flat ones? Or a few square ones? Or a few shaped like triangles?

AN ANSWER FROM THE LAW OF PHYSICS

It is said that the material from which our planets originated began as molten matter and gases, which assume spherical (globe shaped) patterns consistent with the elementary laws of physics-that planets and stars and other heavenly bodies could not assume any other shape than spherical, considering the laws of physics and the character of their composition.

Who was there when the universe was formed from molten matter and gases? No one, you say? Then how can we be so sure? The Creator was there, of course, assuming the claim is sound. But who else? No one!

If the "laws of physics" are credible (and I assume they are) let's ascribe their existence to the God of creation. Scientists claim that a liquid mass in a vacuum will assume a globular, round shape when principally acted upon by its own gravity.

A mastermind must have been behind the creation of our universe and its vast array, whether by the "Big Bang" or by some other route. There's no other logical conclusion. Surely some maker must have made my wristwatch. To think otherwise is to border on insanity.

RIGHTEOUSNESS AND PURITY

Many leaders in the churches of Christ thought developing a relationship with God was accomplished by keeping the rituals and traditions (which we mistakenly thought was scripture) to the "letter." When we base our Christianity on ritual, we spend too much time evaluating other people's performance. If, in our mind, we're outdoing "them," we feel good. We want to feel that we're better than others. And when we do that, we're always looking at others. We decide which people are the extortionist, and the unjust, especially if none of those descriptions fit us. If people on down the ladder measure others this way, the lowest measure becomes the standard. All of a sudden, Adolph Hitler will comfort someone who is at least better than he. This type of comparing is what God would mark as "self-righteous." Mark Twain once said, "Having spent considerable time with good people, I can understand why Jesus liked to be with tax collectors and reprobate sinners." When Jesus said, "Blessed are the pure in heart…" he wasn't talking about ritual but about purity of heart.

In reality, I can't fault my brothers completely. After all, that's the way law operates in society. Keep the laws of your society and you're consider a good, "law abiding" citizen. Unfortunately, the operative principles for a human society are not the same for "kingdom people."

When I pay my income tax, the IRS doesn't give a hoot about whether or not I do it with a good feeling. My motives don't matter. All that matters is that if I owe one thousand dollars, I pay one thousand dollars.

A wife thinks about murdering her husband. She can feel like doing it and think about doing it, but the law will never allow the case to come to court unless she takes an axe to him! A man may want to rape a woman. He can fantasize about what it would be like, but he'll never go

45

to jail thinking about rape. It's only when he commits the act that he goes to prison.

The people of Christ's day, like those in our time, didn't get convicted for their motives, so the main concern was the "letter of the law." But, God was and is concerned with the heart of the matter…and what matters is the heart.

When baseball Hall of Famer Grover Cleveland neared the end of his life, he said, "I have tried so hard to do the right." We may sometimes share Cleveland's thoughts; but as we think about what Jesus had to say about righteousness on the Sermon on the Mount, we have to conclude that we will never be able to throw all strikes. And, even though we may sense our likeness with other people, comparing ourselves with others is the wrong focus. Instead of looking down the ladder, we must start looking up at Him. Looking up begins a cleansing process deep in our hearts.

FATE OF THE UNREGENERATE

BUFF SCOTT, JR.

A few years ago a writer attempted to estimate the number of people who've lived and died since the beginning of the human family in the Garden of Eden. He supposed that if this Earth were one great graveyard, the graves would be twenty deep all over the surface of the planet including mountains and oceans. If his estimate is even close to accurate, just think of the billions and billions of people who have lived and died since the dawn of creation. But, only a small percentage of these billions have been exposed to what might be called special revelation. Is God unmindful of these billions? Is there any hope for them?

It's not our intention to play God. We don't wish to sit upon the Supreme Judgment Seat by advancing the view that many responsible adults who were never exposed to special revelation will presumably be delivered eternally by God's mercy. We favor this position because we're convinced that Deity addresses this question. I don't harbor an insatiable urge to condemn others because they are, or were, unavoidably ignorant of certain facts, events, and truths. It's my position that under certain conditions, God will liberate many who lived and died without a special revelation in the form of an audible or written message.

"Unregenerate" means those mentally competent and responsible men and women who were receptive to truth, any truth, but who died without any opportunity whatsoever of hearing the Good News about Jesus and responding to it. In other words, adults who had no occasion to be exposed to any kind of special disclosure, whether by direct contact with God, Jesus, angels, prophets, apostles-or by way of scripture. We will not address those who were or could have been exposed to some form of special revelation but neglected or refused to accept the opening. They're not included in this study.

Numerous members of the human family from Adam to Moses were exposed to special revelations by way of direct contact with God, angels, or prophets. Heavenly messages in the form of scripture were not available until God commissioned and guided Moses to record decrees, commandments, laws, instructions, and events. Following Moses and up to our present time, many segments of the human family have been exposed to some form of special revelation-whether God, Jesus, angels, prophets, apostles, or scripture. The remainder of humankind has been without such special revelations. But in affirming they have been without special revelations, we don't wish to infer they've been without any revelation. In one-way or another, God has always communicated with His creation. In some ages He chose to communicate with certain peoples and nations in special ways. While the Holy Scriptures are for all of mankind today, there are countless millions who have no access to them. Yet, these millions have a revelation from God through the things He created.

Since the very beginning, God has revealed Himself to every member of the human creation. He has never left his creation without some form of revelation, even those nations and peoples outside of a covenant relationship-such as the Gentiles under Moses and the Old Covenant. God has made Himself known to every kindred and nation under heaven. Every person has been able to "seek Him and perhaps reach out for Him and find Him, though He is not far from each of us" (Acts 17:27). God has, in fact, always been aware of His whole creation, having "determined the times set for them and the exact places where they should live" (Acts

17:26). God is alive in the universe! He knows of and is interested in everyone's plight.

The pagans in the first chapter of Romans were without special revelation. Nevertheless, God revealed Himself to them through the things He created.

"Since what can be know about God was plain to them, because God had made it plain to them. For since the creation of the world God's invisible qualities-His eternal power and divine nature-have been clearly seen, being understood from what He has made, so that men are without excuse. For although they [pagans or Gentiles] knew God, they neither glorified Him as God nor gave thanks to Him" (Romans 1:18-21).

These Gentiles had been given a revelation, but not a special revelation in the form of audible or written messages. They were exposed to Deity through God's creation. They could have even glorified God and given Him thanks, but they chose not to. Although without a special manifestation, they could have served God.

His revelation can be know through His splendid handiwork, for "God's handiwork declares His glory." His invisible qualities are clearly seen in His visible creation. Every mentally competent person who has ever lived has been able to find God, for "he has set eternity in the hearts of men" (Ecclesiastes 3:11). All men, everywhere and in every age, have been divinely infused with awareness of Deity and of life after physical death. On that principle, we must conclude there've been many "unexposed" persons who were receptive to the "revelation of creation." And those who sought God's face, as limited as it may have been, and who "by persistence in doing good sought glory, honor, and immortality, he will give eternal life" (Romans 2:7).

Since God has never required the impossible in any age, it seems to me He will show mercy to those who seek His face, regardless of the revelation under which they have lived or may be living. Note the qualification: Those who seek His face. This is the key. The man in the remotest jungle in Brazil who responds to the only revelation to which he has access-the revelation of creation, although unexposed to scripture and never hearing the name Jesus is glorifying God and will, therefore, be delivered by His mercy and grace. God's creation is the only revelation he knows. He responds to that revelation by trusting in a Supreme Being and giving thanks to Him, as the pagans in Romans could have done.

CORNELIUS

Cornelius, a Gentile, was referred to as a "righteous and God-fearing man" (Acts 10:22 & 35), even before he knew about Jesus and the new Way. But, Cornelius needed additional light. God sent the apostle Peter who revealed a special Light to him and his household in the person of Jesus. Needless to say, many "Corneliuses" have died without coming in contact with that special Light. Such people were acceptable to God, even if they were not His covenant people. To put it another way, wherever there are people like Cornelius there are people acceptable to God.

Martin Luther's parents died Roman Catholics. A friend asked him on one occasion if he believed his parents would be saved in heaven. Luther answered affirmatively. His friend reminded him that he was now opposing Catholicism while believing his Roman Catholic parents would be saved in heaven. The friend goaded him for a clarification of the apparent contradiction. Luther explained that his parents submitted to all the truth they knew or could know at the time, indicating God does not require the impossible. Luther gave a sensible response. When anyone seeks God's face and consistently strives to conform to the only revelation he has, God "will give him eternal life" (Romans 2:7). What else could possibly be required of a man when he responds to the only truth or revelation he knows or can know? Are we ready to exclude him from Paul's decree that "those who by persistence in doing good seek glory, honor and immortality, he will give eternal life" (Romans 2:7)? The man in remotest Brazil does good. He seeks glory, honor, and immortality as best he can, based on the only revelation to which he has access-creation. Paul says God "will give him eternal life!" Read it again. Let us not forget that God does not require the impossible of any man. Considering God's enormous mercy, it seems that eternal condemnation for lack of obedience will not be relegated when opportunity to obey is unavailable.

Jesus touched upon this kind of situation when He taught there is no guilt when one is unavoidably blind of certain truths. The self-righteous Pharisees were chiding Him in their usual way. Following the healing of a blind man, Jesus said He came into the world that those who do not see may see, and that others who see may become blind. The Pharisees asked Him, "Are we blind too" [of certain truths]? Jesus answered:

"If you were blind, you would not be guilty of sin; but now that you claim you can see, your guilt remains" (John 9:35-41).

We can't pass this premise without giving it serious attention. Jesus' seems to be saying:

There is no condemning guilt when one is unavoidably blind of certain truths and facts.

When a man has no occasion to hear of and submit to divine injunctions, and the heart is sincere, there is no convicting guilt credited to his account. In a related passage, Jesus announces:

"If I had not come and spoken to them, they would not be guilty of sin. Now, however, they have no excuse for their sin" (John 15:22).

Will God take vengeance upon those who do not obey the gospel of Messiah Jesus? Of course He will. The divine testimony says so (I Thessalonians 1:8). I'd be the last to deny or defy this truth. The question is, however: Are there exceptions to this divine piece of legislation? I'm compelled to answer in the affirmative. This heavenly principle or truth encompasses only those who have been or can be exposed to the Gospel message. The severely retarded are excluded. The mentally incompetent are spared. Infants and small children are omitted. These three classes alone testify that the celestial legislation is not all-inclusive. I'll even assert it *is* all-inclusive of those for whom it was meant, and I'm referring to those who are competent and have the opportunity to hear the Good

News and embrace it. It can't apply to or include those persons incapable of comprehending the Good News. But is there a fourth class? Let's see.

The three classes referred to above all have insufficient capabilities. They're not expected by man or by God to yield to celestial decrees. I suggest there is a fourth class: Those who are devoid of opportunities. These persons cannot be expected to obey what they have not been exposed to the Gospel message, unless God requires the impossible. Please remember that my premise includes only those unexposed persons whose hearts are honest and receptive.

We're all aware that millions of American Indians lived and died without any opportunity of hearing the name Jesus and responding to His message of salvation. I like to think that some of them responded to the truth they knew or had discovered through God's creation. If some of these Indians served and honored God through the avenue of nature or created things, but could not honor and glorify His Son because of insufficient opportunities, will His blood not reach them through this avenue? His blood reaches those who are incapable because of mental incompetence through the avenue of mercy and grace. I'm confident His mercy and grace will also compensate for the "good Indian" who honored God through nature, but could not accept Jesus and submit to the Good News because of insufficient opportunities.

As was noted earlier, the Gentiles in Romans who had never been exposed to special revelation in the form of scripture, knew God and could have glorified and given Him thanks through His handiwork, "but their thinking became futile and their foolish hearts were darkened." These Gentiles or pagans could not have transgressed Jewish law, or the special revelation God gave the Jewish nation, for they were strangers to the Covenant. "And where there is no law there is no transgression" (Romans 4:15). They transgressed the revelation of creation.

And now for the pivotal question: If, in the end of all things, God considers safe those who lacked capabilities, will He not consider saved those honest persons who lacked opportunities? It is not a question of how

God's righteousness is revealed. We agree it is through Jesus. And every person who partakes of God's righteousness in eternal glory will do so as a result of what Jesus did. No one, absolutely no one, will be saved in heaven separate and apart from what Jesus did. This includes the infant and small child, the severely retarded, and the mentally incompetent. If I understand correctly the divine testimony, they will reach heaven without having believed in and accepted Jesus! Yes, you heard me correctly. You might inquire, "But how may they reach heaven without having come in contact with the blood of God's Son?" They cannot. They are not capable of reaching His blood, but His blood is capable of reaching them! Hear me carefully now. Don't miss a word, please.

His blood reached those saints of old who lived and died under the Law of Moses, although they had no opportunity of formally accepting Jesus as their Savior. So it is with those who have lived and died under any and all laws, whether the "law of nature," the Law of Moses, or the law which prevailed prior to Moses. The blood of Jesus will save those under Moses who trusted in God through the revelation He gave them. The blood of Jesus will save those who were unexposed to the Law of Moses but who trusted in God through the revelation of creation. What is true of one must be true of the other. All who respond to the revelation under which they live, and who seek God, regardless of the age or era, will receive God's grace and mercy in the eternal age to come.

At this point it should be said that those who deliberately sinned and disobeyed God and who lived lives of evil without the Law of Moses, will perish without the Law of Moses. They will perish without the Covenant of Jesus as well. But not because they were unexposed to either Covenant, but because they deliberately and knowingly lived lives of evil, thus violating the "divine nature" God had revealed to them through creation. It is a sobering and disturbing truth that too many of us are prone to take the position that ignorance condemns. Not necessarily, for if ignorance condemns none of us will be saved. All of us are ignorant of some truth. If God condemns eternally the honest unexposed because of ignorance, thus requiring the impossible, how could He be a merciful God? God cares. He understands. He is aware of our plight. His mercy is beyond human comprehension!

SOME RELATED QUESTIONS AND ANSWERS

- Question
  May a person reach heaven without believing in the Person of Jesus?

- Answer
  Yes. Among those who will be in heaven are infants and small children, the severely retarded, and the mentally incompetent. I have also added the "honest unexposed" or uninformed-those receptive to celestial truth.

- Question
  If the unregenerate will be saved, in spite of ignorance, what purpose was served in sending a Savior and the proclamation of that fact?

- Answer
  It is God's intention, through the Good News, to not only save the unregenerate from their fallen nature, but that those who are righteous like Cornelius might be conformed to the image of His Son (2 Corinthians 3:18). This is why we take the saving message to the unregenerate. Those who are not seeking light will not accept it. Those who are seeking more light will accept it.

- Question
  Why take the saving message to the unregenerate if they are saved already?

- Answer
  Why cultivate a field of corn if it can be harvested without cultivation? To make it a better field of corn. We take the saving message to the honest unregenerate because we are thus commissioned, and

because the "elected" ones need to hear and be spiritually cultivated-thereby producing a better harvest.

- Question
  So you believe many of the unregenerate ones are part of God's "elect?"

- Answer
  I believe all who reach heaven, whether those born anew or the unregenerate, are part of God's elect.

- Question
  You seem to be saying the "honest uninformed" will be saved by responding to some divine revelation. Isn't this legalism? Paul says people are saved by grace through faith. Explain.

- Answer
  No responsible person will be saved except on the basis of grace through faith, regardless of the divine revelation under which he lived and died. If I understand the divine testimony accurately, God's grace cannot be applied to a person of accountability without faith. It seems there are two principal schools of thought relating to this subject. Consider them and select the one that best coincides with your doctrinal position.

Here they are:

1) Only those who consciously accept the redemptive acts of Jesus will be saved.

2) Only those who consciously reject the God of creation are lost.

Needless to say, I accept the latter premise.

Conclusion

The principle I've introduced in this essay should be pondered deliberately, namely: Some lack capabilities; others lack opportunities. If God extends grace and mercy to those persons lacking capabilities, will He not grant grace and mercy to those honest persons lacking opportunities?

Does God use one measuring rod for those persons lacking capabilities and a different measuring rod for those persons lacking opportunities? If we limit heaven's population only to those who had the opportunity to hear and respond to divine revelations in the form of audible and written messages, the corridors and airways and arcades of heaven will be mighty empty! I suspect that when we reach heaven we'll find many people there whom we felt would not be there, and quite a few not there whom we felt would be there. It's good that God is the Judge, for we are too prone to misjudge. He understands the predicament of the unexposed. He is not a phantom. He is real! And He will save those who seek Him! The bottom line, however, is that God is still in control, and He will accept or reject whomever He wishes. Praise His Name!

Will the Real 'ekklesia' Please Stand Up?

Some are on welfare, yet some have been monetarily blessed. There are senior citizens as well as twenty-year-olds. Some assemblies have alcoholics as members and some open their arms to those who have no alcohol problems themselves, but family members who do. The one thing they have in common is they all believe that they cannot live fully human lives without a "Higher Power."

They begin their meetings with the "Serenity Prayer," and end them with the Lord's Prayer. "Your will be done...give us this day our daily bread...forgive us as we forgive...deliver us from evil." Perhaps that's all that matters in the end.

They follow a kind of spiritual rule, which consist of not only uncovering their own deep secrets but of making peace with the people they have hurt and been hurt by. They seek help from each other and from books. They sometimes have setbacks. They sometimes make miraculous gains. They cry together. They laugh together. They take special responsibility for one another, agreeing to be available at any hour of the day or night.

Now, for just a minute let's leave Alcoholics Anonymous and talk about something most readers would be more familiar with...God's church. I'm going to be brutally honest with you. So, let me start by saying that I'm having a "lover's quarrel" with God's church!

The contrast between the truth telling of Alcoholics Anonymous and the unspoken rules and hidden agendas in the body of Christ concerns me. Secrets, doubts, and disagreements are kept more or less under cover for propriety's sake. Yet, when I read my Bible, I find truth always spoken in something extraordinary...love. Together they never fail. Anything less turns an assembly of believers into an assembly of strangers. Personally, I need a group that communicates the truth in love, and looks out for one another. I need individuals of faith in my life who confess their setbacks and miraculous gains. People who create an environment where deep secrets can be shared and Satan can be defeated. How about you?

Now, I'll be the first to say that Alcoholics Anonymous is not perfect anymore than anything human is perfect. But, the church of Christ could learn from this group. I'll also be the first to say that what goes on in Alcoholics Anonymous might be far closer to what a first century "ekklesia" looked like. These groups have no buildings, money, located preachers, or pulpits. They make you wonder if the best thing that could happen to the church of Christ today would be for it's building to burn and it's budget to crash.

Just think, all that would be left would be God and each other.

HERMENEUTICS (AGAIN)

What was the hermeneutic of the first century church? Did they follow the contemporary command, approved example, and necessary inference peculiar to the churches of Christ?

Traditionally, we've interpreted the "one faith" to mean the doctrines of the New Testament, specifically the system of belief found between Acts and Revelation. Do we really believe that the early church had a complete set of documents that they could study to determine church organization and practice?

The New Testament wasn't compiled into a single unit until AD 393. In the period between the first century and the fifth century there were at least seven questionable books disputed by the church fathers. Those books were Hebrews, James, 2 Peter, 2 John, 3 John, Jude, and Revelation. For the first four hundred years of the church's life these seven books carried no apostolic authority.

Many Christians in the first and second century only had small fragments of what we know today as the New Testament. Therefore, it would have been impossible for these early believers to live by our contemporary principles of interpretation.

There will always be those who say that the apostles revealed all truth orally until it took written form. But, in some cases, it seems this would be very unlikely. As far we know, no apostle visited Rome until after Paul's letter to that church in AD 57. Shortly after, Nero began persecuting Christians. So, it appears that the church in Rome didn't receive anything close to what we know as a complete revelation of New

Testament doctrines, either orally or in written form. The most they received was a letter from Paul.

Even if the church did receive complete oral teachings concerning doctrine and practice, it could only have been in concise form. Can we safely assume that God intended for these early believers to remember and rely upon oral tradition (as well as utilize the principles of command, example and inference) for four hundred years until the cannon of Scripture was completed?

Did God expect the early believers to interpret Scripture and establish authority the way we have today in the churches of Christ? It seems that our manmade method of ascertaining truth doesn't fit well with our propensity for first-century Christianity.

LET'S PUT THIS IN SYLLOGISTIC FORM.

- Major Premise: The New Testament church had a blueprint to follow in order to be a faithful church.
- Minor Premise: The blueprint was revealed in what we know as the New Testament.
- Conclusion: Therefore, the pattern of the first-century church was found in the New Testament Scriptures.

If either the major premise or minor premise is false then the conclusion is wrong. This short article challenges the rightness of the minor premise.

Tradition and Opinion

THE INFAMOUS SEARCH COMMITTEE

When reading the book of Acts, you certainly never come across a search committee looking for an orator (pastor, point man, evangelist, "fall guy," or hand holder). Search committees are just not a part of the history of the 1st century church, or for that matter, the Restoration Movement. Who is responsible for this infamous idea I don't know. But, it's just that! It's simply a flawed approach that becomes a verbal dance between candidate and committee as each try to be as attractive as possible in this ecclesiastical mating ritual. Discussion can be no more than a few questions and the exchange of pieces of information about one another (with both committee and candidate attempting to reveal their best side). The tragic result is that the hiring congregation and evangelist don't (and can't) really get to know one another until a later date. At best, this means that the first year ("honeymoon-period") is spent discovering the truth. At worst, such a flawed process makes everyone disillusioned when unexpected attitudes, ideas, and commitments don't surface until after the newly hired evangelist arrives.

THE PASTOR SYSTEM

Today, I have no difficulty understanding and discerning the New Testament difference between the work of an evangelist and the work of a pastor. Gene Clemons helped me put flesh on those passages. They became so clear to me as I watched him and then compared his work with what I'd seen and thought was the work of an evangelist. What a difference! He had a way of inviting the local minister to join him on the mission field, insisting that he could put 50 preachers to work. It impressed me that he got such little help and that he had to work with such limited resources.

The "Pastor System" as practiced throughout Christendom today has no biblical basis. None!

So the question begs, "If its basis is not biblical, where did it originate?" The system grew up and out of the events surrounding the Reformation movement. The ex-Catholic priests who became the disciples of Luther were accustomed to seeing the priest carry out the seven pastoral duties.

- Marry the young
- Bury the dead
- Hear confession
- Bless community event
- Baptize babies
- Visit the sick
- Care for and collect money for the poor and the church

Luther instructed these men to continue the pastoral duties of their traditions, but with one slight alteration. He deleted "hearing confessions" for "spiritual counsel and preaching the Bible."

It wasn't long until Luther sent his pastors out to perform the seven (slightly altered) pastoral duties a la Catholic Priesthood, minus the priestly garb and without the "Father" and "Priest" titles. Instead they exchanged their former titles for that of "Pastor."

In all church (denominational) history there has not been so much as one day of debate or controversy over the right of this system to exist. But, let's give credit to the churches of Christ who have denied this system from a theological standpoint. Unfortunately, they fell to its temptation when the system was adopted on an emergency basis during the Civil War in an attempt to prop up the weak condition of the churches after the war. Knowing better, the churches of Christ still practice this anti-Scriptural system.

Why call it anti-Scriptural? For several reasons:

- It interferes with the principle of the priesthood of all believers.
- It supplants the work that God has given the Elders of a congregation to do.
- It supplants the work that every Christian has been called to do.
- It obstructs true evangelism by supposing that it's the minister's work to do the evangelism.

Are we keeping our ministers (evangelists) (preachers) from their proper function by means of this system? What would be the effect if we turned all the Restoration preachers (ministers) (evangelists) loose on their communities in "real" evangelistic work? No longer bothered with office work, or pastoral calls, or sermonizing. Instead, only fishing, fishing for men. Just like Jesus.

EXPANDING A WOMAN'S ROLE?

Would it be fair to call for a reexamining (a rethinking) of what the Scriptures have to say about a woman's role in the church? Or would you consider such a challenge as "anathema?" Is it ever okay to restudy a tradition, teaching or doctrine? Personally, I view any reexamining as a healthy exercise in independent thinking.

Are we willing to rethink the issue of a woman's role with a view toward offering women all the possible alternatives within the parameters of Scripture even if it goes against what we formerly believed?

We need to get rid of a theology that has been limited by the fear of "what something might lead to." Our personal study is going to have to overcome the entrenchment of the past. We are going to have to become, once again, independent and thoughtful and rigorous if we're ever going to determine the context and parameters of Paul's statements regarding a woman's place and role within the body of Christ.

Maybe before we ever ask what the biblical parameters of a woman's role is within the body of Christ, we need to ask some lead questions. Questions like what truly constitutes biblical leadership, authority, and submission?

We may need to consider the possibility that we've supported a double standard regarding what submission in the body means for men and women. For instance, men are to be in submission to one another and to their spiritual leaders. To stand before their leaders, to word a prayer, to read announcements, to sing, even to hand their spiritual leaders a communion tray is never considered a violation of the call to submission. A young Christian boy can do all these things and never once be considered a spiritual leader in his congregation. But we assert that if a woman does any of these things in the presence of men, she violates the principle of submission.

Recently we've begun to address this issue in a limited degree. But we've avoided the call to revisit these scriptures with openness to reevaluation. Our task is to approach the present and the future with an open invitation to revisit the scriptures. To ask questions that we've not asked when our present interpretations were formed. To once again think on our own.

CHRISTIANS ASSEMBLING TOGETHER

As a new Christian I had moments when I'd ask myself, "Why didn't God give us directive scriptures like 'Go to church on Sunday, every Sunday, pray, sing, preach, take the Lord's Supper, return for evening service and then meet again during the week.' Be sure to follow the pattern." Now, years later, study has made it clear to me that God never gave the above instructions to the church. There's not one trace of scriptural evidence that God, an apostle, or any inspired writer ever instructed the church to come together to "perform a worship service." Try preaching that next Sunday.

There are a number of instances in scripture where the early Christians came together, but never for the express purpose of engaging in "items" of worship. Those proof texts we've used to prove that we're the "one true church" were often lifted out of their context. A familiar example is the two passages we've used to show that a cappela music is God's music (Colossians 2:15-16 and Ephesians 5:19). Neither of those passages is even in the context of the assembly!

Yes, we are to assemble, but the primary purpose of our coming together is for "encouraging one another so that we aren't hardened by sin's deceitfulness." (Hebrews 10: 25; Hebrews 2:12)

Why don't we follow the 1st-century example and meet to discuss and take care of problems? Maybe more workers would be utilizing their gift in the body today if we lovingly communicated and worked out our problems instead of ignoring them. Look at some 1st-century examples. There's the man who married his father's wife, and the misinformed Christians who were taking each other to court. These problems were discussed and resolved. Often in Scripture you see the disciples hammering out difficult issues and questions (Acts 15). Certainly there are examples of coming together in scripture, but never to perform public, corporate acts that we call worship.

Let me make it clear that Christians are to WORSHIP! But, worship is not building centered. It's heart centered. Worship is constant. It's everyday, all day, in every act, and every place. It's reverence and submission to the will of God. It's visiting the orphans and widows in distress. It's doing for others what you would want them do for you. It's sincerely caring about the burdens of my brother and sister. It's realizing that God resides in us and that whatever we do to a brother, we do to Jesus. It's being devoted to Jesus and to one another.

Christ-centered worship has more to do with loving and voluntarily surrendering to the Savior and our brother than it has to do with ritual.

PATTERNISM OR A GRACE FAITH SYSTEM?

Many church of Christ members approach the New Testament as if it were a legal document. They search for rules that will allegedly lead them into a correct understanding of all Bible issues. This would be a good idea if the New Testament were a codified legal document and not the "perfect law of liberty." Fortunately Romans 6:14 and Galatians 5:18 testify that we are no longer under the weight of law. Why then, would anyone want to be bound up by law?

Everyone would agree that the Old Covenant was a legal document where commands were spelled out with absolute clarity and directions were made clear. The New Covenant is not a legal system with camouflaged directions requiring legal specialists with special tools to unlock and make known what God expects of us. If the New Testament was a legal document, why did God suddenly stop spelling out in meticulous detail what is necessary and binding? Why would God replace a clearly spelled out legal system with a not-so-clearly spelled out legal system couched in veiled commands, numerous examples which may or may not be applicable, and inferences which may or may not be necessary (depending on who is making the application) and then call it a "better" covenant?

One of Martin Luther's greatest achievements was his German translation of the Bible. Luther prefaced that translation with this statement: "...what to expect in this volume, lest he search it for commands and laws, when he should be looking for gospel and promises." Luther then warned his readers, "Beware lest you turn Christ into a Moses, and the gospel into a book of law."

Patternism has lead to an endless list of church splits and divisions over such trivialities as one communion cup versus multiple cups. The list is endless. The gospel approach will rejoice in remembering the Lord no matter how many cups are used. The law code seeks to justify the individual because right acts are done in right ways. The gospel approach will justify because faith in Christ and His promises bring salvation into a heart, which then acts in loving ways toward his fellow man.

WRITTEN CODE OR
FIRST CENTURY SNAPSHOTS?

Let's imagine for just a minute that the officials in your hometown are ecstatic about a time capsule that's just been discovered in the courthouse lawn. They learn that the chest they have unearthed is four hundred years old. Inside is a collection of articles and documents on the subject of a 20th century game called "baseball." The game is now defunct, but the find stirs the interest of the people. The conversation turns to the possibility of reviving this old "past time." The officials begin studying the documents hoping to learn the rules of the game.

After hours of looking through the documents they learn that there are few details of the game. Most of the documents found in this time capsule are historical accounts of a few games played between the New York Yankees and the Chicago Cubs during the 1980s. Nowhere in the material is an actual list of rules found telling how to play the game. This must be deduced from the available information. Soon, disagreements arise as to interpretation. One example is that there are many references to umpires, but there's no mention of how many are required in a game. Some argue that the game cannot be played without an umpire; others say that only one is necessary. Others argue that there must be at least two.

Other questions arise. For instance, it's clear that the Chicago Cubs didn't play night games. So, it is argued by some that baseball in its purest form can only be played during the day. Others contend that the Cubs seem to be the exception rather than the rule. Several of the documents mention that the New York Yankees used a designated hitter. But there is no evidence that the Cubs used one. Further investigation reveals that there were no females on either team. Therefore, an argument rages over whether or not women should be allowed to play baseball in its restored form.

The New Testament isn't a systematic presentation of rules. It is a set of snapshots of the life, practice, and formation of Christianity in places as varied as Jerusalem and Corinth. Rulebook Christianity attempts to enforce guidelines from the perspective of law rather than from the perspective of Jesus and is the foe of the sufficiency of the gospel of grace.

FENCE THEOLOGY

After carefully contemplating all the risks, the neighbors decided that the chain link fence around their yard inhibited and limited their children. So, they took it down. When the fence was up, the children played right up to the foot of the fence in complete safety, even though a busy street was on the other side. Once the fence was removed, however, the children moved back closer to the house and played. The fence had been their security. When we place adults behind chain link fences often we refer to them as prisoners. What brings freedom to one brings imprisonment to another. To have freedom and to grant it to others is always intimidating.

In the churches of Christ, our "fences" most often define us. They are our "identifying doctrines." These distinctives are our primary source of self-definition and identity. It's unfortunate that outsiders have often recognized us only by what we've emphasized in our preaching and teaching. "You're the ones who don't believe in music" or "You think you're the only ones going to heaven." Sadly, they've not recognized us by how we live (fruits of the Spirit or the primary biblical doctrine of the Lordship of Christ).

Our fences have spawned more denominations than they have united in the 150 years of the American Restoration Movement. Will we ever learn that it's wrong to disparage each other, to caricature those who disagree with us as dishonest or stupid or both. Such arrogance has no place among people who wear the name of Christ. Are we destined to forever be a unity movement creating disunity?

Paul encouraged us to "speak the same thing" (1 Corinthians 1:10-12) as opposed to shouting our different party slogans from across the fence. The phrase "speak the same thing" is a political term describing "unity of allegiance." Our allegiance is not to a thought or a doctrine. These are the materials that build fences. Our allegiance is to the Person of Jesus Christ. He's the "rally pole." He's the one unity is built upon. It's only right that Christians "speak the same" slogans of allegiance to Jesus alone. Jesus was crucified for all believers. He's not divided. Jesus is the common bond and He alone deserves our undivided allegiance.

Have you ever noticed? If someone seeks to dismantle any section of the fence, or to call for a different source (Jesus) of identification, they are either vilified or venerated.

ONE COUNTER EXAMPLE
DISPROVES A CLAIM

Traditionally, churches of Christ have argued that a belief or practice is pleasing to God only if supported by a biblical command, an approved example from Scripture or an inference based upon a premise. This logical attempt is appealing because it seeks to be Biblical. It is also objective and requires a "thus saith the Lord." But, it does have limits of application and interpretation because we humans are fallible. Sadly, many divisions have arisen within the Restoration Movement due to logicians not recognizing those limits. Do I deplore this hermeneutical approach? No. But, this approach is not without some major theological problems.

First, this approach is not found in Scripture.

While it's true that people in the first century probably obeyed commands, drew inferences, and applied examples, they never used the systematized method we're discussing. The Holy Spirit did all the coaching and directing as the apostles and prophets taught the infant church. Our human logic lacks this divinely inspired guidance. When we use the command, approved example, and necessary inference approach, we do things that first-century Christians didn't do.

There's another problem with this approach.

While individual arguments may be developed logically, the system generates conclusions we don't believe. So, if the conclusions are incorrect, something must be wrong with the process that generated them.

A man sat in a stable and watched as seventy-five brown horses were paraded past him. His conclusion, "All horses are brown." To disprove his claim you wouldn't have to gather up all the horses in the world to see if they were brown. All that is necessary is one white horse. That one counter example would disprove his claim.

For years we've argued that the only logical approach to the authority question is through the command, example, and inference hermeneutic. Would your logic allow you to say the system just might be suspect if I can find one counter example?

We've determined that the Lord's Supper should be eaten each Sunday because of two apostolic examples (1 Corinthians 16:2, Acts 20:7). Our conclusion is based upon an unstated command. So far, so good. Logically, however, this system should force us to eat the Lord's Supper in an upper room. After all, Jesus instituted the Lord's Supper in an upper room (Mark 14:15) and the context of Acts 20:7 places the Lord's Supper in an upstairs room. But, we've concluded that an upper room is not an approved example. Since this has been our conclusion, does this example become a counter conclusion? Our human reasoning has said that the Lord's Supper should be eaten each Sunday, but the upper room example doesn't "apply?" Interesting. Wonder why? Who determines what's an approved example? It certainly wasn't a divinely guided logician.

HUMAN-EUTICS?

In the churches of Christ, the stringent COMMAND, APPROVED EXAMPLE, or NECESSARY INFERENCE hermeneutic has determined the categorical approach to the authority question.

This approach in establishing biblical authority has much to commend it. The necessary inference factor, however, has its problems.

FOR EXAMPLE:

1. Who decides what is necessarily inferred and what is not?
2. What determines what is necessarily inferred?
3. Should we listen to men who assign themselves unbelievable power and presumption in legislating from necessary inference?

It's important to understand that there are two kinds of logical inferences. There are *necessary* inferences and *sufficient* inferences. A necessary inference is a conclusion drawn from a premise. If the premise is true, then the conclusion is also true. The method used by a logician to analyze this kind of reasoning is known as *syllogism*. An example of this is:

- All people are rational beings. (major premise)
- All Americans are people. (minor premise)

Therefore, all Americans are rational people. (conclusion)

This type of reasoning guarantees the conclusion (statement #3) to be true, if it is demonstrated that major and minor premises are true. So, it's possible to have a misleading necessary inference.

- All dogs have four legs. (major premise)
- Fido is a dog. (minor premise)

- Therefore, Fido has four legs. (conclusion)

The major premise is not true; therefore, the inference is not true. Let's look at a familiar biblical inference.

- Christians broke bread on the first day of the week (major premise).

- Every week has a first day (minor premise).

- Therefore, Christians broke bread on the first day of every week (conclusion).

NECESSARY INFERENCE OR SUFFICIENT INFERENCE?

If you look closely at Acts 20:6-11 you'll find that verse 7 only says that they "came together to eat bread." It doesn't say that they "ate the bread." They ate the bread in verse 11. So, it is very possible that these disciples ate the Lord's Supper after midnight. And, it's more than probable that they were following Roman time, where the day began and ended at midnight. If not, why would Luke (a Gentile) describe an event in a Gentile town using Jewish time?

Another problem! Does the phrase "breaking bread" refer to the Lord's Supper? Maybe it does, and maybe it doesn't. The phrase "breaking bread" was a Hebrew idiom that meant, "eating a meal." The round flat loaf of bread the Jews ate was not cut. It was broken and pieces torn off from the whole. When Jesus and the disciples ate the Passover, Jesus took the bread and blessed it, then broke it, and gave it to the disciples. In 1 Corinthians 10:16 and 1 Corinthians 11:24, we read the same phrases, "The bread which we break" and "he broke." Granted, they relate to the eating of the Passover and Lord's Supper. But, they are not idioms meaning, "to eat the Lord's Supper."

"Sufficient inferences" are conclusion based upon reasoning know as "inductive reasoning." It can be defined as "an argument which claims only that the premise provides some evidence for the conclusion." A man sits on the street corner of a large city observing the color of automobiles as they pass by. He sees a hundred black cars and no others. His reasoning does not guarantee that his conclusion is correct.

Most of the inferences that we conclude with in our Biblical studies are *sufficient* inferences, not *necessary* inferences.

REASONING I REGRET

I was zealous in my pursuit of the lost. It wasn't unusual for three to four souls to make a decision for Christ (as I taught it) in a month. Then, conversion meant understanding the "five items of worship" and that instrumental music was a sin. I believed this was supported by scripture and was crystal clear. Now, years later, I'm saddened by the "Jesus plus" gospel I once taught. I've since repented of that position.

I'm certain that many of those I taught were converted to "correct" doctrine rather than the Person of Christ! Support for my former position was found in a (nine) New Testament passages and a few Old Testament examples. All that was necessary was an honest heart and the application of good reason and logic.

The story of Nadab and Abihu (Leviticus10:1-3) was a case in point. Nadab and Abihu were two defiant men who did what they knew not to do. Their sin was in defiance of the directives given in Leviticus 16:12-13. The incense was to be burned with coals on the Altar of Sacrifice. Instead of obeying the Lord, they disobeyed Him and burned a different kind of fire than He had commanded. They ignored the commandment that had been given and God destroyed them. Did God put the commandment on record after the fact? I don't think so. It's entirely inconsistent with God's nature. When I read about the God of the Bible, I don't see a blood thirsty God who loves to catch one of His children in an unintentional "goof," so He can lower the boom.

In fact, the rest of Leviticus 10 clearly shows the kind of God that He is. Eleazar and Ithamar, the successors to Nadab and Abihu broke another commandment and rather than zap them with fire, God overlooked their error. Moses was upset, God wasn't. This example also means something.

81

Maybe some of us need to spend more time with the "rest of the story." Nadab and Abihu were my evidence, my "ace in the hole," that I used to prove that God fried all who sang with the instrument. I regret that I went beyond the simple facts of this story in an unfair attempt to teach an unrelated New Testament doctrine.

Another Old Testament story I no longer use is the gopher wood of the Ark. If you look up "gopher" in a Hebrew dictionary, you'll find that it means "resinous" wood, a generic word, which includes pine, fir, cedar, spruce, and hemlock-in short, a wide range of possibilities. I misused and applied this example by asking, "would it be okay if Noah changed the wood of the Ark from gopher to pine, hemlock, cedar or spruce?" When God specifies a kind of wood all others are excluded and when God said, "sing" that excludes playing. My faulty reasoning had given an Ark constructed with anything other than gopher wood (not realizing the broader definition) a quick, short and inglorious career, as well as the soul who sang with a musical instrument.

I believe that God has named the sins and transgressions, which annoy Him and jeopardize our eternal souls. To call something a sin which doesn't appear in the Biblical catalog of sin and then to use reasoning to judge others makes one the god of discernment. Roy Keys has said, "God is not found at the end of a syllogism. If this were true. He would be a conclusion." If, through personal study and conviction, I come to the conclusion that I can't sing with an instrument, then so be it. But to cosign all who use instruments to an eternal Hell is more than just a little presumptuous.

This discussion is not challenging the rightness or wrongness of musical instruments, it is challenging "major premise" leveling, the tool we've used to construct an argument against others and their faith. There's nothing wrong with logic and reason, when the procedures are correct.

HELP ME UNDERSTAND

Our heritage has taught that Scriptural authority is determined by the command, example, and inference formula. Find the commands, look for the examples, induce from the known and then derive by reason. Easy? Well, of course you must sift through the historical details, read between the lines, and then determine which of the many examples are the approved ones. But, use the above formula and voila-you have God's authority on all truth.

First, let me say that this approach isn't found in Scripture. It's true that people in the first century obeyed commands, drew inferences, and applied examples. But they never used the systematic method we're discussing. In fact, they had the Holy Spirit "coaching" the apostles and prophets as they directed the church. Our logic today lacks this inspired guidance. When we use the command, example, inference approach we do things the first century Christians didn't do.

Think of how we appoint elders. We take the information in 1 Timothy 3, add it to the instructions in Titus 1, take out the duplications, and generate an accurate streamlined list for godly men seeking the eldership. While that's not wrong, it's certainly not the way Timothy did it at Ephesus or Titus at Crete. They each had their non-identical, separate Pauline list. Why? Maybe because God wasn't looking for "qualifications" but for "qualities." For now, however, let's agree that Titus 1 and Timothy 3 are where we go to find qualified men to lead God's people.

How does the congregation where you assemble appoint elders after finding qualified men? Do you vote? Or maybe an elder stands before the congregation and makes the often heard announcement, "If there is anyone here who knows any reason why any of these men should not pastor this flock, please let one of the elders know." Is this a Biblical method, or is this man's tradition? Consider Acts 14:23. Here we have two praying and fasting evangelists doing the appointing. Optional? Cultural? Not applicable today? Someone help me understand.

Acts 12 is a familiar story to the Bible student. Peter is in prison, an angel comes to his rescue, chains miraculously fall off and Peter walks to freedom. Immediately, he goes to the house of Mary, where Christians are assembled to pray. When he arrives at the outer entrance, Peter knocks at the door. Rhoda, a servant girl, goes to the entrance, hears Peter's voice, and in her joy leaves Peter standing behind a closed door. With excitement rushing through her body Rhoda runs back into the assembly and announces before all the men and women, "Peter is at the door!" I wonder why it's okay for a female to make an announcement in a 1st-century house church but it is not okay in a 21st-century church building? Someone please help me understand.

SYSTEMATIC GIVING

"Now about the collection for God's people: Do what I told the Galatian churches to do. On the first day of the every week, each one of you should set aside a sum of money in keeping with his income, saving it up, so that when I come no collections will have to be made. Then, when I arrive, I will give letters of introduction to the men you approve and send them with your gift to Jerusalem. If it seems advisable for me to go also, they will accompany me." (1 Corinthians 16:1-4 NIV)

For a decade I watched the church treasurer change the weekly figures on the record board in the church auditorium. It was a no-brainer. Giving to the church budget was a measurement of one's faithfulness to the church and to God. At that time, it seemed reasonable to believe that this was one of the five weekly "items of worship" and an essential part of God's divine plan. But, a more time intensive study of the above passage has led me to believe that this is a mistaken concept we've read into God's word.

It's clear that Paul's instruction in 1 Corinthians 16:1-4 to "set aside a sum of money," was a special collecting and pooling of funds for a 1st-century church in a Jewish world. The question we must ask ourselves is this: Have we taken specific instructions intended for a historical emergency and made it a universal law for all Christians of all times in all places?

While there are many unanswered questions, there are some things we know with certainty.

- Paul's instructions are addressed to *individuals* in the congregation at Corinth.

- These funds are to be put aside on a *weekly* basis

- These monies were *not* used to fund overhead cost or salaries arising from other ministries.

- These Sunday collections were only to help meet a special, temporary need related to congregations in the Jewish world.

- Collections were to be completed prior to Paul's arrival. Once he was there, there was no longer a need for money to be collected.

Concerning 1 Corinthians 16:1-4, Albert Barnes said, "It does not mean that he (Paul) had assumed the authority to tax them, or that he had commanded them to make a collection. But that he had left directions as to the best manner and time in which it should be done. The collection was voluntary and cheerful in all churches."

I've searched the scriptures and have yet to find a command where the Holy Spirit instructs the church to systematically contribute money to a weekly "church treasury." This is a modern day extension of 1 Corinthians 16. Granted, it may be the most expedient way for the church to operate, but let's not use 1 Corinthians 16 as our proof text. It's simply not in the text!

My question for those well-meaning Christians who advocate the "law of exclusion," is this: If you really believe that the silence of the scriptures demands that there be no deviations, additions, or subtractions, why not apply the rule here? It's clear that Paul instructed these Christians to set aside on every first day of the week. Keep in mind that this collection was earmarked for the poor Christians in Jerusalem. What is the basis for using the weekly collection for anything other than benevolence? And on what grounds can these watchdogs say that it's a sin to take up money on any other day except Sunday, when they're not using the weekly collection in the exclusive manner that Paul instructed the early church? It also seems somewhat hypocritical for these patternists to accuse a congregation that gives to a Christian college of deviating from a supposed New Testament blueprint when they themselves "go beyond" the only stated purpose for Bible giving! The supporters of the silence argument have twisted and bent their hermeneutic to fit whatever they want to get into it, while their "law of exclusion" has been freely used to exempt whatever they want to exempt. It all seems more than a bit inconsistent.

Two Thousand Years Later

Two thousand years later, how much do we look like the church in Jerusalem (Acts 2)? Probably about like the fellow who claimed he owned an axe dating back to the days of George Washington. When someone questioned him, saying, "Your axe doesn't look that old," he replied, "Oh, it's that old all right. It's just had three new blades and five new handles. But, other than that, it's the same old axe." That's about how much of what we plea for today resembles the original New Testament church.

Somewhere on our journey, we've fallen into the trap of believing we've restored the church of the New Testament. Let's not forget that restoration is an on going project. It's never finished. It has to be resold and reduplicated in every succeeding generation. This present generation, being the most educated generation in our history, has realized that much of what had been sold as scripture in the past is actually nothing more than the traditions of men. These educated Christians are presently challenging some of our most sacred doctrines. And the baton passers have dug their heels in and taken a defensive position. They aren't aware that their traditions have crystallized into law. They still resist "new words" or "no words" said during a baptism. They continue to label hand raising as rank Pentecostalism, yet ignore plain passages of scripture authorizing it (1 Timothy 2:8). They would faint if someone asked them to send off a missionary by the laying of hands. Divorce and remarriage, the Holy Spirit, and instrumental music continue to produce judgmental attitudes and division in their assemblies.

These things have taken their toll on our numbers and our witness to a lost world. Will we ever learn to disagree without drawing lines in the sand? If the 1st-century church, that we're trying to restore, had followed this path they would never have been "of one heart and mind" (Acts 4:32). No one, other than the Lord Himself, has the qualification or authority to judge.

Maybe we should go back to what the early believers did, and just preach the Word. Let's begin by emulating what the Restoration Movement was founded upon. The freedom to approach the Scriptures individually, without the fear that repudiation will be the consequences of our conclusions.

CAN JESUS SETTLE A 140 YEAR OLD ARGUMENT

Both sides would tell you that they have valid scriptural based arguments for their belief. One side believes that they're right. The other side believes that they're understanding is more logical.

It's a doctrinal difference that caused the non-instrumentalist to turn his back on the instrumentalist for the past 140 years. The issue is mechanical instruments but the underlying (and more serious) problem is the division.

So, we have two sides. The "piano pounders" arguing that they have a choice to use the piano or not, and the "tonsil troops" arguing that the piano pounders are in error for their choice and perhaps going to Hell as well. Which side is right? I certainly have an opinion but that's not to say my opinion is right. I do know what's wrong and it's the division. The solution to the dilemma is in righting the wrong, not in determining which side is right and then having the other side acquiesce.

WWJD? I think, first, Jesus would be very grieved over the past 140 years of separating ourselves from one another. I think He would advocate reconciliation with each side having to give in to their pride-of-theological argument to the humbleness of being a servant to the other side.

Can we resolve a 140 year-old barrier between the non-instrumentalist's theology (which has been unchangeable) and the instrumentalist choice (which is, also, always the same)? Would Jesus give up the right to use piano in order to heal the division? I think He would. I can see Him disassembling all the pianos and nailing them back together as baptisteries, then, commanding the two groups to quit arguing and go into all the world as He commanded. Shame on us.

THE UNITY PLEA

The noble plea for all believers to return to the Bible and unite under Christ was first threatened in 1849 with the formation of the American Missionary Society. The single greatest factor in dividing the Restoration Movement, however, took place in 1851 when a small congregation in Midway, Kentucky, introduced a mechanical musical instrument into the assembly. This division was widened even further with the rise of the slavery issue and the Civil War.

Finally, in 1906, the inevitable happened. For the first time in Restoration history, a religious census officially recognized the Church of Christ and the Christian Church as two separate Christian groups. Today, 150-years later, this division continues.

Both sides sincerely believe that they've remained true to the scriptures. The non-instrumentalist position is that they are right and that the other group made the change, so the division is their fault. The instrumentalist position is that the instrument is simply an expedient, not a doctrine. A century and a half later we're still separated. The unity plea now falls on deaf ears as members of other religious groups, totally puzzled over the "issue," wonder how two groups with a common heritage could be so hostile toward one another.

With that said, let's investigate the position of each side.

INSTRUMENTALIST POSITION

- This group believes that since the New Testament scriptures are silent on the use of mechanical musical instruments, and nowhere prohibited, the use of such instruments is not a violation of scripture. Instruments are used in worship in both the Old Testament and the New Testament. Their understanding of the passage in Revelations 22:18-19 is that it cannot be symbolic, but instead clearly speaks of instruments, so mechanical instruments cannot be an offense to God. Otherwise, they would not be found in temple worship, nor would they be in His home of Heaven, where there is no evil.

- They believe that the Greek word "Psallo" translated *psalm* in Colossians 3:16 and Ephesians 5:19 refers to music written to instrumental accompaniment. This is, therefore, actually a command to worship with instruments.

- The context of Colossians 3:16 and Ephesians 5:19 doesn't refer to the assembly, but the lives of individual believers.[1] Special directives are given to wives, husbands, children, and slaves.

- This group claims there is no difference between tuning forks or pitch pipes and other instruments, such as organs or pianos. They all fall into the category of aids or expedients. If one instrument is a sin in worship, then any instrument is a sin. How many notes are played, or whether it is actually used during singing doesn't matter. One note or a million notes is still sin. They believe the "anti" position is being selective about which instruments are sinful and which are not.

1. Some believe that there is no express authority for singing during corporate worship. From Acts 2:42, four things can be established that the early church did; They kept the apostles doctrine, they continued in fellowship with one another, they broke bread (which probably included both regular meals and the Lord's Supper), and prayed. Other passages reflect these practices, but no passage includes the fifth practice most would include, that of singing in the worship assembly. Zwingli believed everything not based on scriptural precedent should be abolished. Though he possessed considerable musical talents, Zwingli found no authority for singing in the assembly. The Swiss Anabaptist held the same view. Would the silence argument demand, in any way, that any type of singing is unauthorized?

NON-INSTRUMENTALIST POSITION

- This group freely admits to the use of instruments in worship in the Old Testament. They claim that since the New Testament is silent on instrumental music within the assembly that the use of the instrument is an addition to the scriptures and an unauthorized practice. They acknowledge that the Book of Revelation speaks of instruments in heaven. Their position is that these are only symbols, and not real instruments. Therefore they don't apply. They believe that practices in eternity cannot be used only as precedents on earth, since they are two completely different dispensations (Revelation 22: 18-19).

- This group admits that the word "psallo" (translated psalm) meant "music written to be accompanied by instruments." Verses cited are Ephesians 5:19 and Colossians 3:16. Both call for the use of psalms. Their defense is to say that by the time of Christ this word "psallo" came to mean vocal singing only.

- This group claims Ephesians 5:19 and Colossians 3:16 refer to the assembly and they mention only vocal singing. Their position is that instruments are an addition to scripture.

- Some song leaders in the non-instrumental churches use pitch pipes or tuning forks to set the tone of the song. They justify this as acceptable because it is not used during the actual singing.

Both sides claim to accept the Bible as their only authority. Therefore, they have the common ground of scripture. What does scripture say?

- John 17:11, 21, and 1 Corinthians 1:10 are pleas that Christ's people be one. Both sides have been guilty of creating and continuing division-a direct violation of the scriptures they hold so dear. The Corinthian letter was written to a divided church. On careful inspection, one finds that their division stemmed from a failure to understand Jesus (1 Corinthians 1:13-14; 17-18). They were told to correct their mistakes (1 Corinthians 1:2). The only biblical authority an individual or a group of Christians have to withdraw or divide is when scripture, not opinion, is violated.

- While many have tried to prove that Colossians 3:16 and Ephesians 5:19 refer to the assembly, this is a clear stretching of the text. It cannot be sustained.

- None of the verses used by either side justifies the continued division.

- If instruments of music were pleasing to God under the Old Covenant, why are they offensive to Him now?

- When the non-instrumentalist uses tuning forks and pitch pipes they are guilty of contradiction.

The real issue is not scripture, but each group's interpretation of the silence of the scriptures.

THE ARGUMENT OF SILENCE AND PRECEDENT

When it comes to our historic slogan "we speak where the Bible speaks," we've done a reasonable job of teaching what scripture teaches. However, the second half of our motto, "where the Bible is silent, we are silent," is where we've failed.

There should be no argument when the scriptures are silent, after all silence is silent. Therefore, anything said can only be opinion, at best. Unless we have forgotten, scripture is inspired by God not our opinions. Whenever we speak where the scriptures are silent, we take the position that we know exactly what God's position is on that silence.

Thomas Campbell, one of our early Restoration Movement leaders said, "… with respect to the commands and ordinances of our Lord Jesus Christ, where the Scriptures are silent as to the express time or manner of performance, if any such there be, no human authority has power to interfere, in order to supply the supposed deficiency by making laws for the Church; nor can anything more be required of Christians in such cases, but only that they so observe these commands and ordinances as will evidently answer the declared and obvious end of their institution."

Consistency tails off when one leaves the arena of scripture and begins speaking in areas where the scripture are silent For example; the New Testament is silent concerning song leaders and worship leaders. If we're going to use the argument of silence we need to be consistent and do away with this human invention. The song leader and/or worship leader is identical to the functions of an instrument. Both aid in the quality of the singing. And, an aid is an aid-whether human or mechanical.

The argument from precedent says that 1st-century Christians sang exclusively a cappella music. Any change would be foreign to the example set by the early church. Yet, the 1st-century church was without church buildings and Sunday school classes. Are we in violation of 1st-century practices?

The apostle Paul makes the point in 1 Corinthians 10:23 that freedom in Christ is allowed in areas not found in scripture. When we search the New Testament, we don't find a church building. But, this doesn't make it an automatic sin to erect one. Church buildings and Sunday schools fall into the category of unscriptural practices. There's a difference between unscriptural and anti-scriptural. Unscriptural means, "not mentioned in scripture." Anti-scriptural means, "prohibited by scripture." Church buildings are unscriptural, not anti-scriptural.

God doesn't call Christians to violate their conscience (Romans 14:14). What He does call Christians to do is to accept those with different opinions. Are we willing to do this for Jesus? Are we willing to heal the 150-years of division by recognizing that others are not perfect, and neither are we? No one has to accept everything everyone else does or believes. But, we do have to love each other. Just like Jesus loved.

The Emerging

THE EMERGING CHURCH OF CHRIST

THE EMERGING

Change is a necessary and unavoidable reality of life. Often it's welcomed. There are the different seasons, the new baby, and the recent promotion.

At the same time, we hate the change brought about by failing health, social upheaval, and intrusions into our daily routines.

What happens to individuals can also happen to groups of individuals. Change is always challenging. Some want it and others fight it. That's the way we are. The religious leaders resisted the change Jesus represented. So much so, that they crucified Him.

Churches must remain anchored in Scripture; yet change effectively to connect with their culture. It must also be said that change is not always good. The apostle Paul battled change when legalist Christians tried to impose their misdirected will upon the church in Galatia. When churches are caught in the vice of legalism, change is not only right, but also essential. Churches can change for the good as well as for the worse.

Sometime between the early and mid 1900s the movement known as the churches of Christ crystallized. With time, however, she gave up her unique unity plea and settled into an orthodoxy walled about with exclusivism.

Whenever a movement crystallizes there is a polarization that takes place. In the last decade a segment of the movement began to pull away from the exclusive and distinctive doctrines of the right branch of the church of Christ. It was a movement with a sense of purpose and direction. The church of Christ was changing again. But, this time it was a

99

movement that desired to put Christ over and above the party line. Grace was replacing cold orthodoxy. A personal and intimate worship relationship replaced the routine performance of the "five acts of worship."

What's emerging is both interesting and eerie in that the present movement is not unlike the original one. The commonality of the plea is reform through unity. These new restorationist are infused with the original movements passion. Their focal point is built upon the grace and unity of Jesus Christ. These "free agents" of the Lord believe in, and encourage, the freedom to approach the scriptures individually. They understand that inferences from scripture may be true doctrine, but because each Christian is at a different place in their understanding and maturity, these inferential conclusions are not made test of communion. Doctrinal systems have value, but are not made essential to the faith since they are beyond the understanding of many. The oneness plea isn't a "unity of sentiment," but a oneness with a diversity of opinions. It's a movement where forbearance and tolerance are foundational. Where Christians are just as eager to learn from each other, as they are to teach.

CHANGE OR TRANSITION?

Transitions are usually viewed as unwelcome, disruptive, untimely, frustrating, and uncomfortable. They are frequently met with resistance. The present transitional process responsible for the changes we see in the churches of Christ will require a gradual psychological reorientation. This reorientation is necessary to be able to function and find meaning in the new situation. Many people do not clearly understand the difference between change and transition. According to Dr. William Bridges, founder of a management consulting firm and author of *Surviving Corporate Transition*, change takes place at a particular point in time. It occurs when something new starts or something old stops. Change always involves a loss of some kind in a transitional process that culminates in a new beginning.

The human race lives on a continuum of change. No one has all the answers or can speak with infallibility. As long as man thinks, ask questions, and seeks solutions, he will change, both individually and corporately.

EMERGING FROM THE PAST TO THE PRESENT

One hundred years of conflict within our movement has cost us the respect of a divided Christendom. But, even more than that, it has cost the world the gospel!

We've claimed to be "people of the Book." Our "speak where the Bible speaks and be silent where the Bible is silent" aphorism should be more than a quaint motto. The reality of the last decade is that many people in the pews stopped being people of the Book. They've stopped thinking for themselves. It seems that most disputes among us do not arise over what the Bible says. Rather they arise over what some brother teaches the Bible says or does not say.

We've been quicker and more willing to defend traditions worn slick with use than the central truths of God—such as who Jesus is and who we ought to be as a people dedicated to Christ. The underlying theme of scripture is that faithfulness is measured by the centrality of Jesus and the cross in our lives. It's not measured by our adherence to the "policy of the day" as set down by the rigid promoters bent on pushing their interpretations of scripture and who deny that the rest of us are honest in our investigation.

The sad reality of this crystallized movement is that we have implied that we have arrived. We've ceased being interested in restoration as conceived by those we admire as restoration leaders. We've even used the term "The Restoration" as if no one has ever been interested in it but us, and no one will ever consider it again. The simple truth is that we need another restoration. In fact, every generation has the responsibility and the right to put the church they inherited up against the original and trim off the excess. When we stop doing that, we've abandoned the principle of restoration.

There's a current trimming within the churches of Christ that is shaping a grace movement. It has begun to break away from the ruts of traditionalism. There's been a grace awakening in the churches of Christ. The birthing of a new hope that God will use a healed, re-united church once again, just as he did in the early restoration. Watch as the church of Christ emerges!

EMERGING THROUGH TEACHING

One obvious change within the emerging churches of Christ is the new emphasis in their teaching. Realizing that the life, death, burial, and resurrection of Jesus was preached long before the New Testament Scriptures were composed, the movement has turned to a Jesus-centered teaching. A distinction has been made between the gospel of Christ (1 Corinthians 15:1-5) and the doctrine of the apostles. The facts of Jesus can be believed and obeyed by all, but there is room for a variety of opinions and interpretations in regard to the doctrine of the apostles. In the Day of Judgment, there will be no point in bringing God a package of tracts proving our soundness, or dragging in a bundle of arguments that establish our unique "identity." Nothing we bring will see us through that Day. We can only point to the sinless Son of God, slain for our sins and raised for our justification. The eternal truth is that the early Christians were united and enjoyed fellowship well before the New Testament Scriptures were formed. Doctrine has never been the basis for unity. Jesus is the basis of unity. He's the rally pole.

EMERGING EVANGELISM

Mohandas Gandhi once said that if it were only for Christ, he would have gladly become a Christian. Christians kept a great spiritual leader from embracing the Christian faith.

A heresy has been defined as a deviation from an accepted standard within a religious group. Conflicts within a group can take form in three distinct areas. When there's a shift in the accepted doctrinal stance, when there's a departing from Biblical moral standards, and when there's a departure from normal relational standards. Gandhi reacted to the latter of the three. Relational heresy is the greatest obstacle to the spread of the Gospel.

Jesus said that you could judge the genuineness of his disciples by their relationships. "By this all men will know that you are my disciples, if you love one another" (John 13:35). Doctrinal purity is necessary; moral purity is essential; but we can have both without relational purity and fail to be His disciple. Paul described this in 1 Corinthians 13:1-3 when he speaks of three kinds of churches; the doctrinally correct (verse 1), the spiritually gifted (verse 2), and the socially attuned (verse 3). Without relational purity, Paul says, we're nothing.

Through the years we've all experienced random acts of love and kindness within the churches of Christ. But the present emerging is modeling a standard of relational purity that has the potential of demonstrating the transforming nature of the gospel unlike the previous generations. This is key if there is going to be a penetration of postmodern America. For the Gospel message is best proclaimed out of a community of love.

Relational purity is a characteristic that is foundational in the present movements direction.

UNDERSTANDING

According to Paul Tans in his book, "Sign Of The Times," over 95 percent of people who become Christians convert before the age of twenty-five. If this is true, most of our evangelistic growth will come from the generation known as Generation X.

Generation Xers or Baby Busters were born between 1964 and 1983 and are the children of the Baby Boomer generation who were born right after World War II. This generation consists of sixty million Americans. If they were a nation, they would be over one-and-a-half times the population of Canada. They've also been called the "doofus generation" and the "nowhere generation." The buster label stuck because their numbers are smaller than the almost 80 million baby boomers who proceeded them.

As a boomer myself, I'm not proud of what we did to our children's generation. These kids are often the products of divorce, broken homes, a faulty educational system, a government that fails to live up to its promises, and a society bereft of common morality.

For these reasons, Generation Xers possess a troubling list of characteristics, at least from a boomers perspective.

• **Slow to commitment**

Having experienced betrayal throughout their life, Generation Xers have had to deal with the realization that things in which they had placed there hope and trust in: the family, the church, government, technology, and relationships, have all failed to deliver on their promises. The results being that Generation Xers suffer from an overwhelming sense of loneliness.

Because few have seen family commitment in action they understand little about loyalty. Most grew up in dual income homes, meaning that neither parent was very accessible. They learned self-reliance and self-fulfillment at an early age and developed a "look out for yourself and keep your options open" outlook on life. They are ever in search of greener pastures, so they postpone commitments in order to continue evaluating all available options.

- **Distrustful of institutions**

In a recent Group magazine survey, Generation Xers noted that their dislike of the church stems from a distaste for hypocrites, limited thinking, conformity, lack of realism, and cliques. The survey captured some revealing comments: "I know there is a God, but I don't feel I belong in church. The idea is very good, but the church is too political. The actual outcome in today's society isn't practical. Sometimes people worship the form of a religion-this is not God!" Chris Seay says that Xers are "open to the God thing, but not really interested in the church thing" (from Pastor X, Christianity Today, 11 November 1996). Finding spiritual fulfillment is more important to Generation Xers then being involved with the organized church.

- **Indifferent to authority**

The only references many Generation Xers have to Christianity consist of the stories of fallen leaders such as Jim Bakker and Jimmy Swaggart. Unfortunately, both these men represented the Church and Christianity in the 1980s when those in the Generation X age group were in their early formative years. As a result of their "fall" from Christian integrity, as well as other factors, Generation Xers view authority figures within the church and other institutions with contempt and Christianity is all but ignored in the spiritual quest (Dan King in Ministering To Generation X: A Study On Effective Youth Ministry In The 90's).

- **Self-oriented**

The following quote, from a Generation Xer, is revealing.

"If you were to ask most people in our generation about religion, I would guess that many would cite 'disillusionment' with institutions, but probably few could name specific personal incidents that let them down. I think that the problem is just disillusionment in general. Perhaps the solution to finding spirituality in the midst of such built-in cynicism is something that appeals to independent thinkers. Personally, I have discovered that I get the most spiritual satisfaction out of 'alone' moments: hiking, being outdoors, or quiet meditation alone or in a group. I rarely feel enlightened sitting in a large group, listening to someone else theorize (like in church) or discussing my beliefs with others (like in a school setting). I learn more when I think my own way through things. KJS."

Often at the expense of the family, the Generation Xers' workaholic parents worked for work's sake. Generation Xers work to play.

They're not interested in religion, but they are spirituality curious. This curiosity is most often interpreted as being the result of a generation growing up in a post-Christian culture where there's little memory of a hope-giving gospel that can help them face the challenges awaiting them. They realize that there is something spiritual existing in the world, but are cautious about the subject of Christianity. Paradoxically, their values are more aligned with the teachings of scripture than other generations: including importance of relationships, emphasis on family and community, authenticity and servanthood.

Pathways of Denver, Colorado, a rapidly growing, non-denominational church has made an attempt to address the needs of the Generations Xers. This church is a multiracial, multicultural mix of young professionals in there twenties and thirties. They assemble in an older facility that features beautifully stained glass and a large mural of Christ in the temple. These old vestiges of the church have great appeal to the visually oriented Generation Xers. The music is reflective and contemporary. The speaker retells stories from scripture that can last up to thirty minutes. They're high tech but also high touch, contemporary while enjoying nostalgia. They despise lecture, but are attracted to stories. And, even though they grew up with MTV, twenty-second bites and thirty-second commercials, they can handle stories of any length. Yet they tend to tune out the conventional three-point sermon. They learn well in an unpredictable environment. They are visual, prefer low-key dress, are highly experiential, and like to be entertained.

Xers are looking for five main characteristics in faith groups:

- Authenticity—since they have been burned by so many broken promises, they want to know the bottom line and they prefer honesty to politeness.

- Community—they are looking for a true family, unlike the broken, dysfunctional ones in which they were raised.

- A lack of dogmatism—experience is more important than dogma.

- A focus on the arts—where faith can be shared and expressed through various art forms.

- Diversity—racial, economic, and ethnic diversity authenticates Christianity's claim of loving one's neighbor.

The Generation Xers who regularly attend church are usually those who have been exposed to church life at a young age by their boomer parents. Some of these young people are beginning to return to church. And if we are going to keep them, and reach those in their circle of influence, we're going to have to communicate a message that penetrates the head, heart, and will.

Aesthetics, or art, is a movement from the right brain to the left. Consequently, art is often the back door to the left-brain…the side of our brain that analyzes truth. Clearly, this generation will be brought to faith through great aesthetics. The power of art draws people to behold it. Over time they begin to wonder if the ideas that inspire it are true. The emerging churches have recognized that the art of contemporary worship is more likely to attract this generation of non-Christians. Aesthetics is important as an effective means for helping people grasp the truth about God, whether it's through contemporary music or drama. The object is to communicate God's message to the audience of our day in the most effective way.

Unfortunately, the majority of Baby Busters don't attend church. And few, as children, have been exposed to church life. The old answers won't work. We need new ideas and new thinking. We can't sit on our hands and wait for the people to "come to church." We must go to them. Tony Compolo has said that this generation must experience Jesus before they will be ready to listen to the message about Him. Even Jesus' disciples had to spend time with Him before they were ready to hear the Good News.

In the past, we've said, "Come to church with me." People seemed to respond because they had a past which prompted them to seek God again as they were trained to do as a child.

That strategy is rarely effective today and will probably become even less so as time moves on. The emerging church of Christ is well positioned to teach these Xers, but she must incorporate Jesus' methods of teaching if they're going to be reached. How? By going to them.

The religious leaders of Jesus' day would walk miles out of their way to avoid Samaria. Christ not only went to Samaria, but also risked His life there by talking to an adulterous woman in public. The emerging Church of Christ will have to rely less on "church assemblies," and rely more on a willingness to go into the bars, the pool halls, and the coffee houses to befriend those who won't "come to church."

OLD WINE SKINS

A major shift that must emerge in the present movement is to allow the pulpit ministers to step out of the limiting box we have put them in. We have trapped them in a profession that they never signed on for-a career as an institutional chaplain to the church of Christ. Previous leadership required them to be more committed to the institution than to the local community. If we're going to experience the quantity and quality of conversions we read about in the book of Acts, we're going to have to cut the ministers free from the web we've trapped them in. It's the differences between an inward look and an outward focus. If we could interview God, He would say, "What does it profit a church if it keeps all its traditions and keeps its people happy, but loses its soul of compassion for the lost and hurting? Go and announce the good news, love the people and serve them. Deliver them from the hell of their lives." We must emerge!

EMERGING THROUGH MUSIC

Music can be incendiary. Martin Luther said that music is effective in driving the Devil away. Maybe that's why the Enemy makes church music the target of so much opposition. Change the music on a given Sunday and some will sense that their musical turf is being invaded and threatening by "camp songs" for "change sake." Others will cry that change is too slow and that we're capitulating the status quo. Let's be honest. Stretching beyond our personal musical preferences and biases can be risky. Stretching usually hurts at first. But regular stretching causes muscles, even musical ones, to limber up and get stronger.

The new church of Christ is beginning to emerge with some clearly defined, well-focused principles that guide our worship. Our choice of principles over personalities has seen the exit door for the disgruntled few become an entrance door for many more. Our vision for intimate worship seeks to blend a rich a cappella heritage with fresh contemporary expressions.

When God rescued Israel from Egypt, old songs, like old wine skins, could not contain the new energy. So Moses and Miriam sang a new song (Exodus 15). God's special mercy to Mary prompted a new song: "My soul glorifies the Lord and my spirit rejoices in God my Savior." (Luke 1:46-47). Whenever there is renewal in people's lives, there will be new songs just as wine requires new wineskins. The kind of renewal that calls for a new song is not an isolated event but a movement of divine origin.

Emerging Through Drama

The educated and sophisticated audiences of today are so accustomed to graphic information and instant entertainment that the typical three-point sermon does little to make a lasting impression. Television, motion pictures, DVD, computers, and other visual media have tremendously influenced how an audience listens to a Gospel presentation. Throughout the 20th century, the Gospel was successfully communicated by transmitting information through lecture. Today it's become a rather dull affair. The question the body of Christ must ask in the 21st-century is; can we expect to attract and keep today's seeker with rational-centered preaching?

If the Gospel is going to be communicated to the sophisticated audiences of the 21st–century, Christians must overcome these obstacles and devise new means to communicate truth through dramatic, interesting, and entertaining forms. The emerging churches have discovered that brief, dramatic sketches grip people's minds and open their hearts to receive the truth of the Gospel message. More and more restoration churches are using drama to preface, or even replace, the minister's sermons. It's an effective dramatic biblical form designed to illustrate the spoken word and soften the hearts of the listener by providing a vehicle for getting people to identify with the character's feelings and circumstances. When used correctly, it becomes an effective tool to focus people on the crucial issues in life. Once an individual's mind is focused upon a critical need in their own life, it becomes easier to steer them to God and the answers He provides. In addition, drama disarms the reluctantly church visitor, because it demonstrates that those in the church are in touch with real life issues.

The emerging churches aren't afraid of a form that is as old as the scriptures. Jeremiah, Ezekiel, Hosea, and other prophets "acted" out God's message to the people. Jesus used common examples and stories illustrating how the scriptures were meaningful to each person in his own life. The parables of the sower, the mustard seed, the unmerciful servant, the workers in the vineyard, and the lost sheep are only a few examples of how Jesus used stories to illustrate the message from His Father. Why shouldn't the Church use this "visual power" to take the most powerful, life-changing message of the ages to our culture and make a meaningful connection with the hearts and minds of our audiences so that they might consider the life-transforming claims of Christ. Using whatever communication process is the most effective is as biblical as the apostle Paul, who said, "I make myself a slave to everyone, to win as many as possible."

GENDER EQUALITY

A growing number of the emerging congregations within the churches of Christ have grown to believe that when a body of believers refuses to allow a woman to baptize, to lead a small group, to serve communion, or to make an announcement, it is being influenced more by human tradition than by the will of God.

Ten years ago it would have been theological suicide to express such a thought. But times have changed. Today, elders, deacons, Bible teachers, and scholars (who have all confessed to a high view of scripture) are asking questions about women's role in the church. These believers are not challenging Paul's clear teachings on headship. They're questioning our traditional interpretations of Paul's view on a woman's role. Realizing that there are many unanswered questions concerning interpretation and present day application, an increasing number of leaders are calling for a rethinking of gender-defined roles within their congregations.

The result is that more and more congregations are recognizing there biblical given freedom to develop the spiritual gifts of both men and women with new levels of involvement. In doing so, God is recognized as the source of all spiritual gifts and stewardship is accomplished without the appalling loss to God's kingdom that results when half of the church's members are excluded from positions of service.

In scripture there's a shared partnership in which both men and women are provided equal opportunities to service.

- Miriam was a prophetess who shared leadership responsibilities with her brothers, Moses and Aaron (Micah 6:4).

- Deborah was also a prophetess, as well as a judge of Israel.

- Huldah was a prophetess of Israel who spoke words of judgment to a delegation of men including Hilkiah (2 Kings 22:14).

- Anna (Luke 2:36) and the daughters of Philip (Acts 21:8-9) were New Testament prophetesses.

Much has been written about the way Jesus esteemed women to a place of honor far exceeding the social attitudes and customs of the first century. Yet, equally significant is the 21st-century call for the church to rediscover the unity and spiritual equality we have in Christ. For far too long women have been taken for granted and their opinions ignored while our male-dominated churches strike an imbalance and disregard for the complimentary gender roles designed by our Creator.

This struggle for "gender-based" balance is similar to the doctrinal tug-of-war that occurs with all sound doctrine. All truth is held in tension by counter-balancing factors such as law and grace, free will and God's sovereignty, faith, and works. All must be accepted with a "both/and" rather than an "either/or" conclusion. The same is true with the issue of men and women. Both are called to submit to one another, yet men are called to sacrifice their interests for the sake of women in different ways than women are to selectively submit to men.

There's always danger in overcorrecting past mistakes. Spiritual equality isn't the only principle found in the New Testament. We need to remember that the first-century women had authority to prophesy only when they wore a head covering, which in Middle-Eastern culture reflected gender distinction and acknowledgement of male headship (1 Corinthians 11:3-12).

The easiest thing would be to do away with either headship or equality. But, in either case, we would satisfy our minds at the expense of the other side of an important biblical truth.

EMERGING EVIDENCED BY A NEW UNDERSTANDING OF THE HUMAN PREDICAMENT

Churches that are moving forward have accepted the reality of family (physical and spiritual) dysfunction and are beginning to become a part of the healing process. For too long, churches of Christ "shot their wounded" with shame rather than offer the healing arms of Christ's grace and understanding. For too long, we've denied leadership to men with "stains" from their past. We seemed blind to the fact that Moses the murderer was used by God to champion the cause of Israel and David the adulterer was called a "man after God's own heart." It made no difference that Rahab became a part of Jesus' ancestry, or that Peter the denier became a church leader.

I remember sitting in a Bible class a few years ago and listening to a brother joke that maybe Christ hasn't returned for His church because He doesn't want to come back to a dysfunctional bride. While I am not endowed with the ability to judge the validity of this brother's remark, I can say with certainty that his comment reflected the sentiment of that time.

There's been a new awakening among the grace-centered churches of Christ. It's a restored fellowship with a broader vision of God's power to use those whom others have stigmatized. A healing community willing to forgive and forget and even uses their fallen, but now recovered leaders. No longer are pulpits reserved for the perfect, but for the prodigal as well. After all, God's leaders were never chosen on the basis of past infallibility, but present sensitivity to His will.

Our fellowship has awakened to realize that we're all fellow-strugglers in desperate need of Christ's forgiveness. The best of us belongs to the faulty club where nobody throws the first stone. We all have Jezebel and Jesus inside our souls—all of us—and they're never apart. And to ignore those with blemishes of the past, even conspicuous sin, is to simultaneously ignore God's mercy.

Moving Forward or Living With Memories?

We continue to experience enormous structural changes in our country and in our world. It's what the business world calls a paradigm shift-a new way of looking at a "breakthrough." Contemporary change is so rapid that it's difficult to keep track of what's happening, much less figure out how to respond. The only way to cope and be effective is to alter some of the ways we view our culture and the church. When a culture or church doesn't recognize a paradigm shift it forfeits momentum and lives with its memories.

In the early 1960s, the Swiss were the master watchmakers of the world. They were the innovators of the jewel movement, sweep second hands, and mainsprings. They were the undisputed leaders, owning 90% of the world market on fine watches and clocks. All that began to change the day two Swiss Laboratory employees walked into the office of management and challenged the future of the Swiss watch with a new invention, the digital watch. They presented their watch to the Swiss executives as the watch of the future. But lacking any Swiss trademarks it was dismissed as an inferior product. A year later, executives from Texas Instruments and Seiko met these two men from Switzerland at a trade show in New York. They signed a contract, patented the digital watch and the rest is history. Since then, 56,000 of the 62,000 Swiss watchmakers have been placed on unemployment. Today they own less than 10% of the market. This is but one classic case of a paradigm shift that was overlooked because a growing company was conditioned to think that the only watches were their watches. They forfeited momentum and now live with their memories.

Paradigms help us make sense and order of our lives. But when identities, traditions, and old paradigms become barriers for emerging paradigms, progress is stalled. The Jews had a similar paradigm problem in the first century. The rite of circumcision and the Law of Moses were hallmarks of the Jewish religion. When Jesus came He ushered in a new era without a word about circumcision. The Gentiles understood Jesus' silence on the subject as a release from the former requirement. The Jews understood Jesus' silence on the subject as an imperative that things had not changed. Interestingly, the apostles were not clear on the subject themselves. A conference was scheduled in Jerusalem where the leaders engage in lengthy dialogue and debate before reaching the decision that circumcision wasn't to be imposed on Gentile converts (Acts 15). Emotionally, the Jews were still living with the old paradigm, even though intellectually they realized they were living in a new era. They were caught in the struggle between what they knew needed to be done and the emotional conditioning of having done it another way.

For years, the majority of churches in the restoration heritage have functioned out of an outmoded paradigm. Only recently have the contemporary, grace-oriented churches recognized that paradigms have shifted. Realizing the need to connect with their culture they instituted change. The mainline churches[1] have, as far as this writer can tell, done

1. Mainline Church of Christ
    A thought-out belief system
    Strong emphasis on missions
    A strong emphasis on Elders and "control"
    Operational definition of an Elder is a permission-withholding position
    Variation of interpretation from congregation to congregation of who is eligible to be an Elder
    Organized toward smaller congregations
    A legalistic exclusionary dimension of whom "we're not" and whom "we're against."
    Leadership is dependent upon personal persuasion and personality
    Changes in mainline Churches of Christ come through long-term, persuasive ministers who build the power to initiate and see changes through on the basis of tenure, confidence, and personality

two things. First they have had a difficult time discerning tradition and opinion from scripture. This misunderstanding coupled with the fear of "going too far," has lead them to settle into the tried traditions of the past. Unfortunately, tradition is a subtle addiction that will eventually lead to mainline demise. So, what does the Holy Spirit seem to be saying to us in this matter? The danger in all this is that we're farther apart today than at any other time in our 200-year history. A WE versus US mentality has developed with the first group seeing the second as a threat and the second seeing the first as "out of touch."

Old paradigms must give way to the new. When we hold on to the old we squeeze the lifeblood out of our congregations, our young people, and young families. The changes the mainline churches must make are no greater than those the Jews were being asked to make at the Jerusalem conference in the first century. Yet, Satan is crafty. He realizes that more is needed than an acknowledgement for change. Recognizing the time for change is essential to a paradigm shift. That's the mistake the Swiss watchmakers made. They understood the need for change. They had already changed by putting sweep second hands on their watches and by putting jewels in them. When given the opportunity to make the major change that was needed, however, they didn't seize the moment and lost their momentum.

THE REALITY

Reunion of the Restoration Family remains a hope for tomorrow. It's not likely to happen in an all-at-once merger in a compromise worked out by leading spokesmen. Nor will it be the result of surrender by one branch recognizing the superiority of the other. It will occur instead when individual Christians recognize that the oneness of Christ body transcends the dividing barriers of sectarianism.

Anton Chekhov set his drama, "Three Sisters," in nineteenth-century Russia where there was a lack of idealism and challenge, and a prevalence of pessimism and apathy. Toward the end of the play, a major character expresses a cautious hope for the future that sounds similar to what many are praying for within our heritage.

> "It seems quite hopeless for a lot of us, just a kind of impasse…and yet you must admit that it's gradually getting easier and brighter, and it's clear that the time isn't far off when the light will spread everywhere…in the old days the human race was always making war. Its entire existence was taken up with campaigns, advances, retreats, victories…but now all that's out of date, and in its place there's a huge vacuum, clamoring to be filled. Humanity is passionately seeking something to fill it with and, of course, it will find something some day. Oh! If only it would happen soon!"

EPILOGUE

A counselor tells the story of his son coming into his office one day and sighing, "Will I always be a skinny person?"

The father told him, "Your destiny as a teenager is to be a string bean maypole. But you can look forward to the day when you walk into this office, hand me your jacket, and say, "Get lost, Dad.""

One day the son walked into the office, handed the jacket to the father and said, "Get lost, Dad." The father put on his son's jacket. The sleeves were too long and the shoulders too wide.

Life is about growth. And growth demands new ideas and challenges. When your ear is to the ground you'll feel the nudges and gentle shoves. This is what this little book is all about. It's a wake up call to the challenges of the truth of Scripture. A call for the churches of Christ to be courageous and take the richer road, even though it's filled with the danger of potholes and hairpin curves.

Sometimes, I struggle with this call. It can make me uneasy when a brother says, "I'm sorry about your error. I'll pray for you." Yet all of this is necessary when paths are being cleared for the future disciples who will respond to the gentle nudges of their faith.

I've chosen to wrestle with the call and to rejoice in each new victory. How about you?

—Fred Peatross

Printed in the United States
32478LVS00003B/64

9 780595 139118